D1006697

DISCARD

Black Women
Activists

Black Women
Activists

Other books in the
Profiles in History series:

❧   ❧   ❧

Black Abolitionists
Leaders of the Civil Rights Movement
Terrorist Leaders

❧

Black Women Activists

Profiles · in · History

Karin S. Coddon, *Book Editor*

Bruce Glassman, *Vice President*
Bonnie Szumski, *Publisher*
Helen Cothran, *Managing Editor*

GREENHAVEN PRESS ®

THOMSON

GALE

San Diego • Detroit • New York • San Francisco • Cleveland
New Haven, Conn. • Waterville, Maine • London • Munich

THOMSON
GALE

SAN JUAN ISLAND LIBRARY
1010 GUARD STREET
FRIDAY HARBOR, WA 98250

Cover credit: © David Turnley/CORBIS
Library of Congress, 17, 21, 62, 127, 146, 152, 160

LIBRARY OF CONGRESS CATALOGING-IN-PUBLICATION DATA
Black women activists / Karin S. Coddon, book editor.

Black women activists / Karin S. Coddon, book editor.
    p. cm. — (Profiles in history)
Includes bibliographical references and index.
ISBN 0-7377-2313-0 (lib. : alk. paper)
    1. African American women political activists—Biography. 2. Women, black—Biography. 3. Civil rights movements—United States—History. 4. Civil rights movements—United States—Sources. 5. African Americans—Civil rights—History. 6. African Americans—Civil rights—History—Sources. 7. Anti-apartheid movements—South Africa—History. 8. Anti-apartheid movements—South Africa—History—Sources. I. Coddon, Karin S. (Karin Susan). II. Series.
E185.96.B538 2004
323'.092'396073—dc22   2003067531
[B]

Contents

Chapter 1: Ida B. Wells-Barnett

1. Ida B. Wells-Barnett

Ida B. Wells-Barnett was a teacher and journalist who lobbied tirelessly for antilynching laws in the post–Civil War United States.

2. A Groundbreaking Journalist

As a newspaperwoman and a pamphleteer, Wells-Barnett called attention to the epidemic of racial violence in America.

3. Burned Alive

Wells-Barnett decries the fact that vigilante mobs have tortured and murdered blacks while countless white bystanders looked on in approval.

Chapter 2: Winnie Mandela

1. Winnie Mandela's Troubled Life

Winnie Mandela's political ambitions have made her a polarizing figure in South Africa. Her alleged involvement with a series of crimes have seemingly tarnished her heroic stature.

Chapter 4: Black Women and the Fight Against Racial Segregation

also participated in the NAACP and voter registration drives.

Chapter 5: Voting Rights, Women's Rights, and Speaking for the Voiceless

Foreword

Historians and other scholars have often argued about which forces are most influential in driving the engines of history. A favorite theory in past ages was that powerful supernatural forces—the gods and/or fate—were deciding factors in earthly events. Modern theories, by contrast, have tended to emphasize more natural and less mysterious factors. In the nineteenth century, for example, the great Scottish historian Thomas Carlyle stated, "No great man lives in vain. The history of the world is but the biography of great men." This was the kernel of what came to be known as the "great man" theory of history, the idea that from time to time an unusually gifted, influential man or woman emerges and pushes the course of civilization in a new direction. According to Carlyle:

> Universal History, the history of what man has accomplished in this world, is at bottom the History of the Great Men who have worked here. They were the leaders of men, these great ones; the modelers . . . of whatsoever the general mass of men contrived to do or to attain; all things that we see standing accomplished in the world are properly the outer material result. . . . The soul of the whole world's history, it may justly be considered, were the history of these [persons].

In this view, individuals such as Moses, Buddha, Augustus, Christ, Constantine, Elizabeth I, Thomas Jefferson, Frederick Douglass, Franklin Roosevelt, and Nelson

Mandela accomplished deeds or promoted ideas that sooner or later reshaped human societies in large portions of the globe.

The great man thesis, which was widely popular in the late 1800s and early 1900s, has since been eclipsed by other theories of history. Some scholars accept the "situational" theory. It holds that human leaders and innovators only react to social situations and movements that develop substantially on their own, through random interactions. In this view, Moses achieved fame less because of his unique personal qualities and more because he wisely dealt with the already existing situation of the Hebrews wandering in the desert in search of a new home.

More widely held, however, is a view that in a sense combines the great man and situational theories. Here, major historical periods and political, social, and cultural movements occur when a group of gifted, influential, and like-minded individuals respond to a situation or need over the course of time. In this scenario, Moses is seen as one of a group of prophets who over the course of centuries established important traditions of monotheism; and over time a handful of ambitious, talented pharaohs led ancient Egypt from its emergence as the world's first nation to its great age of conquest and empire. Likewise, the Greek playwrights Sophocles and Euripides, the Elizabethan playwright Shakespeare, and the American playwright Eugene O'Neill all advanced the art of drama, leading it to its present form.

The books in the Profiles in History series chronicle and examine in detail the leading figures in some of history's most important historical periods and movements. Some, like those covering Egypt's leading pharaohs and the most influential U.S. presidents, deal with national leaders guiding a great people through good times and bad. Other volumes in the series examine the leaders of important, constructive social movements, such as those that sought to abolish slavery in the nineteenth century and fought for human rights in the twentieth century. And some, such as the one on Hitler and his henchmen, profile far less constructive, though no less historically important, groups of leaders.

Each book in the series begins with a detailed essay providing crucial background information on the historical period or movement being covered. The main body of the volume consists of a series of shorter essays, each covering an important individual in that period or movement. Where appropriate, two or more essays are devoted to a particularly influential person. Some of the essays provide biographical information; while others, including primary sources by or about the person, focus in on his or her specific deeds, ideas, speeches, or followers. More primary source documents, providing further detail, appear in an appendix, followed by a chronology of events and a thorough, up-to-date bibliography that guides interested readers to further research. Overall, the volumes of the Profiles in History series offer a balanced view of the march of civilization by demonstrating how certain individuals make history and at the same time are products of the deeds and movements of their predecessors.

Introduction

Historically, black women activists have had to confront a double challenge in their fight against prejudice based on gender and race. In some instances, as occurred both in mid-nineteenth- and mid-twentieth-century America, their precarious balancing of racial and gender identity has been a source of tension within the progressive movement, with black women activists debating whether their primary political objective should be racial or sexual equality. As African Americans, black women have participated in the ongoing struggle against the legacies of slavery and Jim Crow that denied citizens the right to vote, equal employment and educational opportunities, and even from drinking from the same water fountains as whites. Decades before the emergence of the modern feminist movement, black American women, forced first by slavery, then poverty and racist social policies, confronted sexual discrimination in the workplace. In a world where equality has yet to be realized, countless black women activists continue to refuse the status of "second-class citizen" to which history has repeatedly sought to relegate them both because of their race and their gender.

Black Women Activists in the American Abolitionist Movement

Abolitionism, which emerged in the first decades of the nineteenth century, was the first major American social movement in which both black and white women played prominent public roles. Although most of the leaders of the antislavery movement were male, such notable white women as Harriet Beecher Stowe (author of *Uncle Tom's Cabin*), Quaker feminist Lucretia Mott, and leading suffragists Susan B. Anthony and Elizabeth Cady Stanton also lobbied tirelessly for the abolitionist cause as writers, lecturers, and organizers. Along with these well-known white activists, black women continued to agitate for the antislavery cause and for women's rights.

Most black women abolitionists were, like their white sisters in the movement, strong advocates for women's suffrage as well. Yet black women often found their white counterparts ambivalent about pursuing both goals with equal fervor. The woman suffrage movement, like abolitionism, was a subset of a broader trend toward social reform during the nineteenth century espoused by progressive intellectuals and activists. But as the sectional and political divide between slavery's supporters and opponents grew dangerously volatile in the 1840s and 1850s, some white suffragists became leery about wedding their cause too closely to that of emancipation. Organizers of an 1851 women's rights convention in Akron, Ohio, were reluctant to allow black activist Sojourner Truth to speak, for example, lest her presence appear to confuse the issues of female voting rights and abolition of slavery. Although Truth did speak, her small victory could not efface the fact that black and white feminists would be at cross-purposes in pursuing their objectives, a notion that would arise time and time again over the next 150 years.

Division over the "Woman Question"

Even the ultimate triumph of abolitionism, the Thirteenth Amendment that forever banned slavery in the United States in 1865, did not quell the evident divergence in the progressive movement over black and female political rights. Following close on the heels of the Thirteenth Amendment's passage came the debate over black suffrage and whether progressive reformers ought to couple the issue with the "woman question," as the matter of women's voting rights was commonly termed. Once again Sojourner Truth made a forthright entreaty for the inseparability of the two goals, speaking at the American Equal Rights Association in 1867:

> There is a great stir about colored men getting their rights, but not a word about the colored woman; and if colored men get their rights, and not colored women theirs, you see the colored men will be masters over the women, and it will be just as bad as it was before. So I am for keeping the thing going while things are stirring; because if we wait till it is still, it will take a great while to get it going again.[1]

The "thing," of course, was the general post–Civil War sentiment, at least in the triumphant North, in favor of social progress. The nation had taken a tremendous step in eradicating slavery; could equal rights for women as well as blacks be far behind? But others in the progressive reform movement advocated a more cautious approach. Even the great black abolitionist leader Frederick Douglass believed that securing voting rights for black men should take precedence over woman suffrage. The debate culminated in the 1867 enactment of the Fifteenth Amendment, which guaranteed (at least in theory) the right to vote for black men but not for women of any color.

Many feminists felt bitter and betrayed by their former colleagues in the abolitionist movement. Desperation and disenchantment led Susan B. Anthony and Elizabeth Cady Stanton, the two preeminent feminists of nineteenth-century America, to accept for their cause the patronage of eccentric entrepreneur George Fran-

Three African American women protest segregation. Racial discrimination in the form of Jim Crow laws was especially rampant in the South throughout the 1960s.

cis Train, an ardent supporter of women's rights and an equally outspoken opponent of black suffrage. Just as had occurred in Akron with the controversy over permitting Sojourner Truth to address the equal rights convention, African American women activists found themselves faced with the dilemma of conflicting political identities. Should they now dedicate their energies to furthering the cause of equality for blacks, or should they pursue equality as women, a group many feminists argued held even fewer legal and political rights than black men?

Jim Crow and Racist Stereotypes
It soon became clear, however, that the Fifteenth Amendment was not only a partial victory for the forces of so-

cial equality but also a hollow one. Strict segregation in the form of "Jim Crow" laws (named after a demeaning black character in a minstrel show) was enacted to enforce blacks' social inferiority and deter men from exercising their legal right to the ballot. In a practice that endured well into the height of the modern civil rights era, southern blacks were not permitted to travel in the same train cars, dine in the same eating establishments, or attend the same public schools as whites.

The Early-Twentieth-Century Civil Rights Movements

At the dawn of the twentieth century the early civil rights movement in America was beginning to take organized shape. Scores of black women joined the campaigns for racial justice. Many participated in the 1896 founding of the National Association of Colored Women (NACW) in Washington, D.C. The NACW's historical formation laid the groundwork for what would turn out to be a full century of activism by African American women. As historian Dorothy Sterling has remarked in reference to the 1890s, "Black women had always belonged to church and literary societies, but not since antislavery days had they organized in large numbers for political action."[2] Although most of its founding members were also dedicated to the cause of woman suffrage, the NACW was primarily committed to racial equality, service to the black community, and promotion of a positive image of African American women. Journalist and author Lynne Olson describes the gender-specific context of the NACW and its mission:

> In the minds of many female activists in the 1890s, black men had fallen short in the fight for racial justice, doing little more but talk about it. An editorial in the NACW newspaper, *Women's Era*, urged "timid men and ignorant men" to stand aside. This was a

"woman's age," NACW leaders felt, a time for black women to assume leadership in promoting the advancement of their race. Many black men, however, took emphatic exception. John Hope, the president of Atlanta Baptist College, for one, chided members of Atlanta's women's clubs for their "brow-beating spirit" and the "caustic remarks" they had made about men, and charged the women with being "more masculine than feminine." Black men should be encouraged to assert their authority and demonstrate their masculinity, Hope declared, adding that "the surest way for our men to become more manly is for our women to become more womanly. In other words, women should focus less on assuming leadership in the fight against racism and concentrate more on supporting their men.[3]

Regardless of the flagrant racial inequities that characterized black-white relations in post–Civil War America, women of both races were exhorted by traditionalists to define themselves chiefly as "helpmates" to their men.

The fact that poverty and discrimination had forced most black women to work outside their homes made them appreciate keenly the importance of education for African Americans of both sexes. Whereas young black women recognized education as imperative to achieving economic independence, early twentieth-century white women regarded higher education as an option primarily for the upper classes.

In 1909 Ida B. Wells-Barnett and Mary Terrell helped to found the National Association for the Advancement of Colored People (NAACP). Headed by W.E.B. Du Bois, the NAACP was initially conceived by its cofounder, white philanthropist Mary White Ovington, as an interracial as well as gender-inclusive organization. Although by the 1930s the group had become almost exclusively African American in membership, from its inception the NAACP allowed black women not only to belong but also to serve in leadership positions. Among its most influential activists were Ella Baker, who traversed the South during the 1940s to recruit new members; Daisy Bates, president of the Arkansas NAACP, who agitated for desegregation in the Little Rock public schools during the 1950s; and Rosa Parks, whose refusal to yield her bus seat to a white man in Montgomery, Alabama, on December 1, 1955, was a watershed moment that ushered in the modern civil rights movement.

Along with Baker, Bates, and Parks, countless African American women braved intimidation, beatings, and death threats from southern racists determined to cling to Jim Crow segregation and discrimination. Black women participated in organized protests, boycotts, and voter registration drives, demanding full social and political rights for African Americans. Many, such as Fannie Lou Hamer, were arrested and jailed for their activism. Yet despite the willingness of black women activists to risk their families, livelihoods, and even their lives for the cause of racial equality, they were often relegated to the sidelines by their male counterparts in the movement. Such was the case when Martin Luther King Jr. led hundreds of thousands of black Americans in the March on Washington of August 1963 that culminated in a rally before the Lincoln Memorial. Despite their exceptional contributions to the movement, women activists were marginalized and silenced, as Lynne Olson observes: "No woman marched down Constitution Avenue with Martin Luther King, Jr., Philip Randolph, Roy Wilkins, and the rest of the male civil rights leaders. No woman went to the White House afterward to meet with President John F. Kennedy."[4] A hastily improvised "Tribute to Women" at the Lincoln Memorial introduced a handful of female activists, including Parks, Bates, and Gloria Richardson, to the throngs of

NAACP office workers in Detroit organize a membership drive in the 1940s. African American women helped to found the organization in 1909.

marchers, but none of the women was permitted to speak. Not unlike the male critics of the NACW in the 1890s, a significant number of black men in leadership positions seemed to prefer that black women play a subordinate role in the civil rights movement.

Black Women and the Feminist Movement

The prevalence of sexism in both the civil rights and antiwar movements of the 1960s led many female activists to embrace the new wave of feminism, or women's liberation, that was also sweeping across the United States. Three black women participated in the 1966 founding of the National Organization for Women (NOW): attorney Pauli Murray, who coined the term *Jane Crow* to denote the double prejudice faced by African American women; union activist Aileen Hernandez; and New York state assembly-woman Shirley Chisholm, who became the first black woman elected to the U.S. Congress two years later.

Yet tensions soon simmered between black and white feminists over the values and assumptions that shaped the burgeoning women's movement. Many black feminists grew uneasy about what they viewed as women's liberation's predominantly white middle-class and upper-middle-class frame of reference. Sexual freedom, reproductive rights, and the choice to seek employment and self-fulfillment outside of the domestic realm were major objectives of NOW and other mainstream feminist movements during the 1960s. Most African American feminists agreed with the principles, but for a few the priorities seemed those of—and geared to—white educated women. Working outside the home had long been a necessity of survival for black women rather than a means to self-fulfillment. As for the other pillar of constraining Victorian femininity, sexual repression, for generations black women had been fighting a different stereotype—that of sexual wantonness. With the majority of black Americans still living in poverty, "self-actualization" struck some African American women as a luxury, the attainment of which was secondary to the more pressing needs of their working-class sisters.

The National Black Feminist Organization (NBFO), which lasted only two years (1973–1975), was formed as a result of a shared sense among many prominent black women that NOW was insufficiently responsive to the social and economic situation of those outside of the white middle class. With NOW, the NBFO supported the Equal Rights Amendment and women's greater political participation and representation. But the NBFO also emphasized issues of particular concern to poor and working-class women of color: the rights of domestic workers, equitable and effective welfare services, and the disproportionate number of black female victims of forced sterilization and sexual violence. Political-science scholar Duchess Harris comments on several of the NBFO's key distinctions from NOW:

> The NBFO disseminated information on how to reach out to black women, and how to educate them about feminism. The organization placed great emphasis on the need to include lesbians and incarcerated women in their educational and recruitment activities. This was very different from NOW, which had other priorities. The women of NBFO aimed their activities at the more personal and practical level than at the political mainstream. Given their lack of access to the larger political system, it is likely that they saw these issues and concerns as having more of a direct effect on most black women in the United States.[5]

The NBFO was short-lived, dissolving under the weight of ideological conflicts and accusations from some black activists that the organization privileged gender equity over racial equity. The Combahee River Collective, a more explicitly radical-socialist offshoot of the NBFO based in Boston, lasted only until 1980. But like their forebears—Sojourner Truth and the founders of the NACW—black feminists of the 1970s, regardless of organizational affiliation (or lack thereof), held fast to the conviction that racial and sexual justice were inseparable.

Black Women Activists Today

Both in the United States and around the world, black women activists continue to struggle on two fronts, dealing with prejudice born both of racism and sexism. The 1980s saw a new, demeaning stereotype emerge in American political discourse, that of the shiftless "wel-

fare queen," compounding the long-standing stereotypes of the "Mammy" and the sexual wanton. In the
1990s black women have had to combat their negative
representation in much rap and hip-hop music as
"bitches" and "hos." Yet black women have also made
remarkable gains in the public arena, due in part to the
efforts and determination of previous generations of activists and role models. Government and policy scholar
Linda Faye Williams points out encouraging statistics
demonstrating that

> at the close of the twentieth century, the proportion
> of black elected officials who were women was
> greater than the proportion of white elected officials
> that were women. . . . One must conclude that de-
> spite being disadvantaged by not only gender but
> race (and for the most, class), black women have been
> able to overcome political disadvantage within the
> black community more quickly than white women in
> the white community. In sum, although black women
> have clearly not achieved descriptive status (they re-
> main underrepresented compared to their share of
> the population at every level of government), their
> striking electoral progress is one clear legacy of the
> Civil Rights–Black Power Movement.[6]

Indeed, in 2003 Carol Moseley Braun, the first African
American woman to be elected a U.S. senator (1992–
1998), followed in Shirley Chisholm's notable footsteps
by declaring her candidacy for the Democratic presidential nomination.

In the United States black women have distinguished
themselves in many professions—Nobel laureate novelist
Toni Morrison, television personality and media mogul
Oprah Winfrey, Oscar-winning actress Halle Berry, and
children's rights activist Marian Wright Edelman to
name a few. Most of these women have publicly stated
that they view their successes as victories for all women of
color. The twenty-first century promises to offer its own

rich gallery of brave black women engaged in the world-wide struggle for justice, equality, and human rights.

Notes

1. Sojourner Truth, address to the American Equal Rights Association, New York City, May 9, 1867.

2. Dorothy Sterling, *Black Foremothers: Three Lives.* New York: Feminist Press/McGraw-Hill, 1979, p. 96.

3. Lynne Olson, *Freedom's Daughters: The Unsung Heroines of the Civil Rights Movement from 1830 to 1970.* New York: Scribner, 2001, p. 43.

4. Olson, *Freedom's Daughters*, p. 13.

5. Duchess Harris, "From the Kennedy Commission to the Combahee Collective: Black Feminist Organizing, 1960–1980," in *Sisters in the Struggle: African American Women in the Civil Rights–Black Power Movement*, ed. Bettye Collier-Thomas and V.P. Franklin. New York: New York University Press, 2001, pp. 280–305.

6. Linda Faye Williams, "The Civil Rights–Black Power Legacy: Black Women Elected Officials at the Local, State, and National Levels," in *Sisters in the Struggle: African American Women in the Civil Rights–Black Power Movement*, ed. Bettye Collier-Thomas and V.P. Franklin. New York: New York University Press, 2001, pp. 306–31.

Profiles · in · History

Ida B. Wells-Barnett

Ida B. Wells-Barnett

Alfreda M. Barnett Duster

Despite the twin victories of 1865—a hard-won Union triumph in the Civil War and passage of the Thirteenth Amendment permanently abolishing slavery—Reconstruction ushered in another phase of the black American struggle for equal rights. Radical Republican efforts in Congress to enact harsh punitive measures against the former Confederacy and actively promote the welfare of newly freed slaves were defeated, leaving most southern blacks in a position of virtual, if not literal, slavery, dependent on meager sharecropping and subject to the hostility of whites that often culminated in violence. The Ku Klux Klan, a white supremacist vigilante organization, claimed as its ostensible purpose the protection of white southerners from both vicious Yankee occupiers and "uppity" blacks intoxicated by liberty and looking for trouble. In truth, the Klan was a terrorist group whose function was to intimidate, harass, and abuse blacks, often to the point of murder by lynching. By the end of the nineteenth century, thousands of black men had died from lynching across the United States. Leading the charge against lynching and the white apathy that largely ignored it was teacher, publisher, and activist Ida B. Wells-Barnett (1862–1931). The following selection profiles Wells-Barnett, the daughter of former slaves who

Alfreda M. Barnett Duster, *Crusade for Justice: The Autobiography of Ida B. Wells*. Chicago: University of Chicago Press, 1970. Copyright © 1970 by the University of Chicago. All rights reserved. Reproduced by permission.

dedicated her adult life to fighting racism, discrimination, and violence against black Americans.

Herself a lifelong activist for racial equality, the author of the following viewpoint, Alfreda M. Barnett Duster (1904–1973), was the daughter of Wells-Barnett.

❧   ❧   ❧

"**G**od has raised up a modern Deborah in the person of Miss Ida B. Wells, whose voice has been heard throughout England and the United States . . . pleading as only she can plead for justice and fair treatment to be given her long-suffering and unhappy people. . . . We believe that God delivered her from being lynched at Memphis, that by her portrayal of the burnings at Paris, Texas, Texarkana, Arkansas, and elsewhere she might light a flame of righteous indignation in England and America which, by God's grace, will never be extinguished until a Negro's life is as safe in Mississippi and Tennessee as in Massachusetts or Rhode Island."

This statement by Norman B. Wood in 1897 was not an unusual description of this fiery reformer, feminist, and race leader during her lifetime and after her death. In newspapers, magazines, journals, and books of the period from 1890 to 1931, Ida B. Wells-Barnett was described over and over again as militant, courageous, determined, impassioned, and aggressive. These were uncommon terms for a person who was born to slave parents—and who was herself born a slave—in the hilly little town of Holly Springs, Mississippi, in 1862. Her mother was a deeply religious woman whose convictions about the essential dignity of man developed under the cruelties of slavery. Her father, a man of independent spirit even in slavery, sought and attained his full independence in the period following emancipation. These qualities of her parents fused to add fire and zeal to the character of Ida Wells.

Holly Springs had progressed from a small cotton plantation community of the 1830s until by the time of the Civil War it was described as a small architectural paradise. An iron foundry and the main office of the Mississippi Central Railroad made it a much desired location. Although little fighting took place there during the Civil War, the town changed hands many times. During one period of Union possession, Confederate forces under the command of General Earl Van Dorn rode into town, met with little resistance from the surprised Northerners, and burned and destroyed the business section of town as well as the armory and all federal supplies. Many fine homes were also burned or used by soldiers and wrecked after occupation.

Early Life and Education
In this relatively peaceful small town, Ida grew up, living in the home built and owned by her father, with the duties and responsibilities of the eldest daughter of a family of eight children. Her father was a skilled carpenter and had plenty of work rebuilding homes, industrial plants, and government buildings destroyed during the hostilities. He was a man of considerable ability and much civic concern, and was selected as a member of the first board of trustees of Rust College.

Rust, originally named Shaw University, was founded in 1866 by Rev. A.C. McDonald, a minister from the North, who served as its first president. In the early days, Rust College provided instruction at all levels and grades, including the basic elementary subjects. Among the more enlightened portion of the white community in Holly Springs there was support for this college, as was evidenced by the annual report for 1875:

However hostile to the education of the Freedmen the whites may be elsewhere in the South, here both teachers and pupils are respected and encouraged by the most influential of them. One of the first men of this place, an ex-slave holder, has voluntarily taken it upon himself to raise means for us among his people.

Both of Ida's parents stressed the importance of securing an education, and at Rust she had the guidance and instruction of dedicated missionaries and teachers who came to Holly Springs to assist the freedmen. Ida attended Rust all during her childhood and was regarded as an exceedingly apt pupil. On Sundays her religious parents would permit only the Bible to be read, so Ida read the Bible over and over again.

Consequences of the Epidemic

In 1878 a terrible epidemic of yellow fever struck Holly Springs. Two thousand of the town's population of 3,500 fled; most of those who remained contracted the disease, and 304 died. Both of Ida's parents and their youngest child, Stanley, ten months of age, died in this epidemic. Another child, Eddie, had died a few years earlier, and Eugenia, the sister next to Ida, died a few years later. Although friends, neighbors, and other well-wishers offered to take some of the children, Ida, at sixteen, was steadfastly determined to keep the family together. Her father had left some money, and with the help of the Masons, who were guardians, she cared for all of them.

After passing the teacher's examination, Ida was assigned to a one-room school in the rural district about six miles from Holly Springs. As her brothers Jim and George grew into their late teens, they were apprenticed to carpenters and learned the trade of their father, which they followed all their lives.

About 1882 or 1883, an aunt, Fannie Butler, sister of

Ida's father, who lived in Memphis, Tennessee, some forty miles away, suggested to Ida that she move to Memphis and seek a teaching position there. Mrs. Butler, widowed in the epidemic of 1878, offered to care for Ida's younger sisters, who were near the age of her own daughter. Ida accepted and at first taught in the rural schools of Shelby County while she studied for the teacher's examination for the city schools of Memphis.

A Legal Challenge to Segregation

In May 1884, as Ida was on the way to her school in Woodstock, Tennessee, the conductor on the Chesapeake and Ohio Railroad told her she would have to ride in the smoking car. She refused. When the conductor and baggage man attempted to force her to ride in the other coach, she got off the train at the next stop, returned to Memphis, and sued the railroad. The case attracted much attention because whereas the law stated that accommodations should be separate—but equal— railroad personnel had insisted that all Negroes ride in the smoking car, which was not a first-class coach. In December 1884, the local court returned a verdict in favor of Ida Wells and awarded her five hundred dollars in damages. The railroad appealed the case.

Ida did not give up her resistance to the railroad's policy of forcing Negroes to ride in the separate but *unequal* coaches. In her diary she wrote about going with three friends on one of the educational excursions for teachers: "Of course we had the usual trouble about the first class coach, but we conquered."

The victory was short, however, for on 5 April 1887 the Supreme Court of Tennessee reversed the decision of the lower court. At the time she wrote:

> The Supreme Court reversed the decision of the lower court in my behalf, last week. Went to see Judge G [Greer, her lawyer] this afternoon and he

tells me that four of them [the judges] cast their personal prejudices in the scale of justice and decided in face of all the evidence to the contrary that the smoking car was a first class coach for colored people as provided for by that statute that calls for separate coaches but first class, for the races. I felt so disappointed because I had hoped such great things from my suit for my people generally. I have firmly believed all along that the law was on our side and would, when we appealed to it, give us justice. I feel shorn of that belief and utterly discouraged, and just now, if it were possible, would gather my race in my arms and fly away with them. O God, is there no redress, no peace, no justice in this land for us? Thou hast always fought the battles of the weak and oppressed. Come to my aid at this moment and teach me what to do, for I am sorely, bitterly disappointed. Show us the way, even as Thou led the children of Israel out of bondage into the promised land.

Ida Wells, Teacher

By the fall of 1884 Ida had passed the qualifying examination and been assigned as a teacher in the Memphis city schools, where she taught for seven years. During these years, she was regarded as a competent and conscientious teacher, devoted to helping young Negroes acquire what she knew was crucially necessary for their future—a good education. She took advantage of every opportunity to improve her own academic skills with private lessons from older teachers and those skilled in elocution and dramatics. She attended summer sessions at Fisk University and traveled on excursions for teachers to places of interest and value.

Outside the classroom Ida was a serious young woman, scorning frivolities and contemptuous of the wiles that other young women used to attract men. At this time in her life, she has been described as "a very beautiful young woman." Her refined and ladylike appearance did not suggest that she was destined to defy mobs and become a vigorous crusader against the injustices that beset the Negro people in the post-Reconstruction days in the South. She had many admirers and enjoyed going to concerts, plays, lectures, church meetings, and social affairs. In the days when Sunday afternoons were social hours, many young suitors called on her and took her for walks or rides. She was called hard-hearted and incapable of loving anyone, but this was a facade; underneath she longed for the true love of a man she could respect and admire.

Turning to Journalism

In 1887 she began writing for a church paper, using the story of her suit against the railroad and its results as her first article. Soon her articles spread to other church papers and then to some of the Negro weeklies. Thus she discovered her journalistic abilities, and when she was offered an interest in and the editorship of a small newspaper in Memphis, the *Free Speech and Headlight*, she accepted and invested her savings to become part owner. It is not surprising that her articles criticizing the Memphis board of education for conditions in separate colored schools led to her dismissal as a teacher in 1891.

Dismayed but undaunted, she worked diligently on the paper. She shortened its name to the *Free Speech*, and was enjoying her work and travels for the paper when, on 9 March 1892, three young Negro businessmen were lynched in Memphis. She turned her scathing pen on the lynchers and on the white population of the city who allowed and condoned such a lynching. An angry mob wrecked her press and declared that they would have lynched her if she had been found. She had gone to Philadelphia to cover a convention for her paper and was warned not to return. But her pen would not be silenced. She continued her efforts for the cause in the *New York Age*, where she bitterly railed against the evil of lynching. It was about this time that she began to lecture in the northeast. Through this activity she received an invitation to tell the story in England, Scotland, and Wales. She spent April and May of 1893 in this first crusade abroad.

While informing the English people about lynching in America, Ida B. Wells learned of the progressive activities of English women, and she was very much impressed with their civic groups. When she returned to the United States she emphasized the activities of British women to her New England audiences. She urged her female listeners to become more active in the affairs of their community, city, and nation, and to do these things through organized civic clubs. The idea found favorable response and thus the first civic club among Negro women, the Women's Era Club, was organized in Boston, Massachusetts, with Mrs. Josephine St. Pierre Ruffin as president. Miss Wells organized other clubs in New England, and in Chicago she organized the first civic club among Chicago's Negro women. When she returned to England on her second speaking tour, the Chicago group obtained a charter and named the club in honor of Ida B. Wells.

Her Work with Other Black Leaders
In 1893 she turned from the problem of lynching to the slight that Negroes had received at the World's Columbian Exposition. Petition after petition for participation in this Chicago World's Fair had been made by individual Negroes and by groups, but all had been denied. Consequently, during July 1893, in conjunction with Frederick Douglass, Ferdinand L. Barnett, and I. Garland Penn, she produced an eighty-one-page booklet: *The Reason Why the Colored American Is Not in the*

World's Columbian Exposition—The Afro-American's Contribution to Columbian Literature. The preface stated:

> To The Seeker After Truth:
>
> Columbia has bidden the civilized world to join with her in celebrating the four hundreth anniversary of the discovery of America, and the invitation has been accepted. At Jackson Park are displayed exhibits of her natural resources, and her progress in the arts and sciences, but that which would best illustrate her moral grandeur has been ignored.
>
> The exhibit of the progress made by a race in 25 years of freedom as against 250 years of slavery would have been the greatest tribute to the greatness and progressiveness of American institutions which could have been shown to the world. The colored people of this great Republic number eight millions—more than one-tenth of the whole population of the United States. They were among the earliest settlers of this continent, landing at Jamestown, Virginia in 1619 in a slave ship, before the Puritans, who landed at Plymouth in 1620. They have contributed a large share to American prosperity and civilization. The labor of one-half of this country has always been, and is still being done by them. The first credit this country had in its commerce with foreign nations was created by productions resulting from their labor. The wealth created by their industry has afforded to the white people of this country the leisure essential to their great progress in education, art, science, industry and invention.

Continued Travel and Activism

In 1894 Ida B. Wells made a second journey and crusade through England. During this tour of six months, the *Chicago Inter-Ocean* regularly published her articles in a column entitled IDA B. WELLS ABROAD. Her lectures were well received in England, where the press and pulpit gave enthusiastic support to her pleas. An Anti-

Lynching Committee was organized which consisted of some of the foremost citizens of Great Britain.

Returning to America in July 1894, she continued the crusade by lecturing throughout the North and organizing antilynching committees wherever possible. She took up residence in Chicago and in 1895 published *A Red Record: Tabulated Statistics and Alleged Causes of Lynchings in the United States, 1892–1893–1894.* In the first chapter, "The Case Stated," she wrote:

> The student of American sociology will find the year 1894 marked by a pronounced awakening of the public conscience to a system of anarchy and outlawry which had grown during a series of ten years to be so common, that scenes of unusual brutality failed to have any visible effect upon the humane sentiments of the people of our land. . . .
>
> It becomes the painful duty of the Negro to reproduce a record which shows that a large portion of the American people avow anarchy, condone murder and defy the contempt of civilization.
>
> These pages are written in no spirit of vindictiveness, for all who give the subject of lynching consideration must concede that far too serious is the condition of that civilized government in which the spirit of unrestrained outlawry constantly increases in violence, and casts its blight over a continually growing area of territory. We plead not for the colored people alone, but for all victims of the terrible injustice which puts men and women to death without form of law. During the year 1894, there were 132 persons executed in the United States by due form of law, while in the same year, 197 persons were put to death by mobs who gave the victims no opportunity to make a lawful defense. No comment need be made upon a condition of public sentiment responsible for such alarming results.
>
> The purpose of the pages which follow shall be to

give the record which has been made, not by colored men, but that which is the result of compilations made by white men of the South. Out of their own mouths shall the murderers be condemned. For a number of years the *Chicago Tribune*, admittedly one of the leading journals of America, has made a specialty of compilation of statistics touching upon lynching. The data compiled by that journal and published to the world January 1st, 1894, up to the present time has not been disputed. In order to be safe from the charge of exaggeration, the incidents hereinafter reported have been confined to those vouched for by the *Tribune*.

A booklet of one hundred pages, the *Red Record* was not only the statistical record of lynchings in the United States, but a detailed history of the lynching of Negroes—and others—since the Emancipation Proclamation. Her alarm over the growth of mob violence had prompted her to appeal to world opinion. In her crusades in the United States and Great Britain and in her writings she hoped to eradicate this form of barbarism.

Ida Wells and Ferdinand Barnett

The decision to make Chicago her home was influenced by a romantic interest in Ferdinand Lee Barnett, founder of the *Conservator*, the first Negro newspaper in Chicago. Mr. Barnett was a graduate of the law school which later became affiliated with Northwestern University. Years later, Langston Hughes recorded the marriage and noted the mutual interests of the Barnetts as follows:

> In 1895 Ida B. Wells married another crusader, a Chicago newspaper man, Ferdinand L. Barnett, and together they continued their campaign for equal rights for Negro Americans. They broadened their field of their activities, too, to include every social problem of importance in the Windy City where they lived.

Attorney Barnett was a widower. His first wife, Molly Graham Barnett, died when their children, Ferdinand L. Barnett, Jr., and Albert Graham Barnett were four years and two years of age. Barnett's mother had lived with him and cared for the boys during the seven years before his marriage to Ida B. Wells. Four children were born to this union. Charles Aked, born in 1896, was named for one of the leaders of the antilynching crusade in England, the Reverend Charles F. Aked. Herman Kohlsaat, born in 1897, was named for H.H. Kohlsaat, a famous restaurateur and one of the strongest supporters of the Barnetts' civic activities and their newspaper the *Conservator.* Ida B. Wells, Jr., was born in 1901, and Alfreda M. was born in 1904.

The Wells-Barnett Family Life

After the birth of their second son in 1897, Ida B. Wells-Barnett gave up the newspaper and devoted herself to the tasks of homemaker and mother. She firmly believed in the importance of the presence of a mother in the home during her children's formative years. She did not take any work outside the home until the youngest child was eight years old and able to attend school alone. Even then, she arranged for her daughters to spend the noon hour at home under the watchful guidance of a cousin.

She was a kind and loving parent, but firm and strict. She impressed upon her children their responsibilities, one of the most important being good conduct in her absence. There was never any need to be concerned when she was present. She did not have to speak; her "look" was enough to bring under control any mischievous youngster.

Both parents emphasized education for their children. Ferdinand, Jr., was graduated from Armour Institute (now Illinois Institute of Technology). Albert G.

graduated from Kent College of Law, and in his later life was city editor of the *Chicago Defender*, Charles Aked was a student at Wendell Phillips High School when an altercation with one of the teachers caused him to quit school. He left home and secured a job as a chauffeur in Milwaukee, Wisconsin. Later he had his own printing business and worked as printer and layout specialist for other printing firms. Herman became his father's associate in the law firm of Barnett & Barnett. In the depression days he left Chicago, "went West" and served in the California State Employment Service until retirement. Ida was her father's secretary and companion until his death in 1936. Alfreda received the Ph.B. degree from the University of Chicago in 1924, was active in parent-teacher associations, social and civic organizations, and was on the staff of the Division of Community Services of the Illinois Youth Commission until her retirement in 1965.

Within the city of Chicago, the Barnetts exerted influence in most civic affairs. They were perhaps the first Negro family to move east of State Street, when in 1901 they bought a home at 3234 Rhodes Avenue. Although there was no violence when they moved there, they were subjected to various displays of hostility. The white family next door would get up from seats on the front porch whenever the Barnetts appeared, shake their rugs with disgust, and go into their house, slamming the door with displeasure. Within the next decade, as the number of Negro families in the area increased, the Barnett boys and other Negro boys were regularly attacked by the Thirty-first Street gang. As a protective measure, they organized all the Negro boys of the area into a tight group which then met fisticuffs with fisticuffs. On one occasion, when a large number of white youths followed the boys home and stood outside the house jeering and threatening, Mrs. Barnett repeated the assertion that she frequently made during her antilynching crusades: that she had but one life to give, and if she must die by violence, she would take some of her persecutors with her. She kept a pistol available in the house and dared anyone to cross her threshold to harm her or any member of her family.

Still Working for Change

Ida Wells-Barnett never gave up her militancy or dedication to the cause of helping right the wrongs against Negroes. She urged the young men in a Sunday school class she taught at Grace Presbyterian Church to form an organization for this purpose. It was called the Negro Fellowship League and was located at 2840 S. State Street in the area of the largest incidence of crime, wholesale arrests, and "third degree" methods of obtaining confessions. In the three-story building the league utilized the lower floor for the center and the upper floors for sleeping rooms for men without homes— at twenty-five cents a night. In 1914 the league moved to 3004 South State Street, utilizing only one large room for activities for the center, for meetings, religious services on Sundays, and an employment office on weekdays. Even this activity closed down early in 1920, as lowered income and Mrs. Barnett's failing health necessitated longer absences from the offices.

In 1910 when she established the Negro Fellowship League, Mrs. Wells-Barnett hoped for support from middle- and upper-class Negroes with education, ability, and influence. She sought the kind of financial help and cooperation from these Negroes that [social worker] Jane Addams was able to secure from whites for Hull House [in Chicago]. In this she was disappointed. Although her friends and associates in clubs, churches, and social life admired her dedication and hard work, they were not willing to venture into the area of Twenty-eighth and State Street to work among the recent migrants—uneducated, unemployed, and living in such undesirable neighborhoods. Some individuals and some of the federated clubs, such as the Gaudeamus Civic and Charity Club, did give assistance, but it was most inadequate for the urgent needs.

Added to her differences with the upper-class Negroes over service to the unfortunate was her disdain for the crudities she observed among some of them. She felt that the upper class should consist of persons of refinement, good breeding, and good manners. Thus, she resented the entrance of persons of questionable morals who had enough money to pay their way into society.

In like manner, Ida B. Wells-Barnett had high standards for ministers of the gospel and felt that they should be above ordinary men in their personal and professional lives. Any hint of scandal in their personal habits or handling of finances was enough for her to withdraw her respect and support. She thought that ministers had a very special opportunity to reach large numbers of people and that they had a responsibility to use their contacts for the good of those people. She believed that they should assist them in their improvement in this world as well as prepare them for the next world. Many ministers felt that she meddled too much in their sphere of influence, although they admired and respected her dedication to the causes she espoused. In many instances they allowed her to use their facilities for mass meetings and civil assemblies.

The Power of a Voice and a Pen

She continued to fight—with voice and pen—every form of injustice and discrimination in Chicago and anywhere in the United States. During the years of the race riots, whenever reports of them appeared in the daily press she went into action. First she would appeal to organized groups such as the Equal Rights League, the Afro-American Council, the People's Movement, founded by Oscar De Priest, either or both of the political party organizations, the daily press, and the weekly press. She would call mass meetings at churches, at the headquarters of the Negro Fellowship League, or at any hall available to her. Then, with funds secured from personal sources or raised by public subscription or advanced by newspapers—principally the *Chicago Defender*—she would travel to the scene of the riots, make her investigation, and return to Chicago to report the facts as she had gathered them. Her reports appeared in the Negro papers such as the *Defender, World, Broad Ax*, and *Whip*, and in the pamphlets printed and distributed by the Negro Fellowship League. Unfortunately these pamphlets and other letters and documents gathered during her long and eventful career were lost in a fire in her home, and efforts to find copies have proved fruitless. Some of the most notorious of the incidents she covered were the Springfield, Illinois, riot, the Elaine, Arkansas, riot, the Helena, Arkansas, riot, and the riot in East Saint Louis, Illinois.

In December 1920 she was hospitalized and underwent surgery. She attempted to get about too soon and had a relapse which kept her quiet for most of that year. As she regained her strength, however, she moved again into the mainstream of civic, political, and, to a lesser extent, social life in Chicago. She became an active member of the National Equal Rights League and the local Chicago chapter. She was elected again—after a lapse of thirty years—as president of the Ida B. Wells Women's Club, which she had organized in 1893. In addition, she began a campaign of lecturing to enlist support for a most active, dynamic, and effective National Association of Colored Women. This program met with some success, but also with much opposition.

In her zeal to effect change she did not mince words or spare the feelings of those whom she decided were "do-nothings."

In 1924, at the club's convention in Chicago, she entered the race for president against Mary McLeod Bethune, who had served as vice-president, but was unable to gain enough support to be elected. Disappointed, but still conscientiously concerned about the club work among women, she continued to participate in the Ida B. Wells Club, the American Rose Art Club, the Chicago and Northern District Association of Club Women, and the State Federation. She also maintained her connection with the club work among white women of the city through the Cook County Federation of Club Women.

She continued to lecture to groups throughout Illinois and the country whenever requested to do so. From Jacksonville, Illinois in 1920 she wrote:

> They have arranged for me to speak here tomorrow (Sunday) night at one of the churches. The conference of Charities and Corrections which I came to attend is moving along smoothly. I was at the State School for the Blind, also for the Deaf yesterday, and was greatly interested. [I spoke] at a meeting arranged for me last night. They had a good house, and they want me to stay over and make another speech. I cannot get out of here until Monday morning which will keep me traveling most of the day, reaching home in time for dinner Monday night with my loved ones.

Political Values

Throughout her life she had great faith in the power of the ballot and worked unceasingly to stir citizens to register and vote. Although women's suffrage was still only a hope, she urged men to use the ballot for their defense and protection. As early as 1910 she wrote an article "How Enfranchisement Stops Lynching" in the *Original Rights Magazine*. When the opportunity was given the women of Illinois by the general assembly, a very limited franchise which allowed women to vote for trustees of the University of Illinois, she was among the first to urge women to take advantage of this right of citizenship. She organized the first suffrage club among Negro women on 30 January 1913, calling it the Alpha Suffrage Club. In the small one-sheet newsletter, *The Alpha Suffrage Record*, she wrote:

> Chicago, as we have said many a time before, points the way to the political salvation of the race. Her colored men are colored men first—Republicans, Progressives and Democrats afterwards. In the last twenty years, on but one spot in this entire broad United States has the black man received anything like adequate political recognition and that one spot is Chicago. The corollary of this proposition is that on only one spot on this broad United States have colored citizens demanded anything like adequate political recognition and that one spot is Chicago.

Both Ferdinand L. Barnett and Ida B. Wells-Barnett were politically loyal to Charles S. Deneen, a leading Illinois Republican. When he was state's attorney, Deneen had appointed Mr. Barnett assistant state's attorney—he was the first Negro to hold such a position, and he kept it for fourteen years. Meanwhile Mr. Deneen progressed to become governor, then United States senator. He split with the regular Republican organization and headed the Deneen faction of the Republican party until his death in 1940. The Barnetts believed that the Deneen faction had higher principles than the regular organization. However, in 1930 Ida B. Wells-Barnett became a candidate for state senator, running as an independent against Warren B. Douglas, who was supported by the Deneen faction, and Adelbert H. Roberts, who was supported by the regular Republican organization. She came in a poor third. She stated, "Few women responded as I had hoped." Again disappointed, but undaunted, she wrote in her diary:

> Have been unable to have a conference with my backers, so we may profit by lessons of the campaign. . . . Am issuing cards for Tea Sunday 5–25 [1930] which is also a letter of thanks to those who helped. . . . Spoke at Orchestra Hall to a large white meeting, and at the La Salle [Hotel] to a luncheon at which all the candidates spoke.

A business card identifies her as national organizer, Illinois Colored Women, and on the reverse side in her handwriting a form for a proposed ticket to "The Women's Republican League Whist Party."

At Metropolitan Community Church, which she joined immediately upon its founding in 1920 by Rev. W.D. Cook, former pastor of Bethel A.M.E. Church, Mrs. Wells-Barnett was teacher of an adult Sunday school class and president of the Forum. The Sunday evening Forum presented outstanding speakers and engaged in discussions of religious, civic, and social importance. After the Reverend Mr. Cook's death, she continued to carry on many programs under the ministry of Rev. Joseph Evans.

Later Years

By 1925 both sons and the younger daughter had married and established homes elsewhere. Young Ida, unmarried, still lived at home and worked as her father's secretary in his office at 111 S. Dearborn Street. The fourteen-room house on Grand Boulevard, renamed South Parkway, was too large for the family of three; so they took a five-room apartment at 326 East Garfied Boulevard.

In 1927 or 1928, Ida B. Wells-Barnett became increasingly aware of the importance of recording the facts concerning her activities during the antilynching crusade and the troubled times from 1893 to 1927. So in 1928 she began to write her autobiography. Painstakingly she wrote, rewrote, revised, and corrected the manuscript. The first third she wrote by hand, then, securing the services of the secretary of her son, Attorney Herman K. Barnett, she dictated the rest, carefully proofreading and revising. The final chapter of her autobiography illustrates the fact that every item of injustice or discrimination brought the militant and crusading spirit to the fore and made her move to "do something" about whatever the matter happened to be.

On 21 March 1931, she went downtown to do some shopping. In the evening she complained of not feeling well and spent Sunday in bed. On Monday morning she was incoherent and obviously very ill. After a hurried family conference, she was rushed to the Dailey Hospital where Dr. U.G. Dailey and a group of consulting physicians attempted to save her life. Uremic poisoning had progressed too far, and without regaining consciousness, she died on Wednesday, 25 March 1931, the birthday of her eldest son, Charles. In tribute to her memory, the *Chicago Defender* described the woman Chicago had known as "Elegant, striking, always well groomed . . . regal."

The few papers and diaries and the autobiography on which she had been working have remained in the possession of her family since her death.

Her Legacy

Ida B. Wells will be remembered most for her fight against the lynching of Negroes, and for her passionate demand for justice and fair play for them. In the preface to her autobiography she mentions that a young lady compared her to Joan of Arc. The analogy is, at best, strained, but the odds against her were in many ways even greater. True enough, Joan was a peasant girl in a time when peasants and girls had nothing to say to the ruling class of France. But Ida B. Wells was a black woman born into slavery who began openly carrying her torch against lynching in the very South bent upon the degradation of the blacks. Joan had the advantage of rallying a generally sympathetic French people to a common patriotic cause. Ida Wells was not only opposed by whites, but some of her own people were often hostile, impugning her motives. Fearful that her tactics and strategy might bring retribution upon them, some actually repudiated her.

The memory of Ida B. Wells-Barnett has been kept alive in several ways. There are Ida B. Wells clubs in various parts of the country. In 1950 the city of Chicago designated her as one of the twenty-five outstanding women in the city's history. The followers of this leader of women spearheaded the drive which secured for her the most significant recognition that she has yet received. In 1940, through an intensive campaign conducted by women's clubs and civic and social organizations, the Chicago Housing Authority changed the name of the South Parkway Garden Apartments to the Ida B. Wells Garden Homes. Covering forty-seven acres and housing seven thousand persons, the Ida B. Wells Homes primarily serve that portion of the population that she had served throughout her lifetime.

The most remarkable thing about Ida B. Wells-Barnett is not that she fought lynching and other forms of barbarianism. It is rather that she fought a lonely and almost single-handed fight, with the single-mindedness of a crusader, long before men or women of any race entered the arena; and the measure of success she achieved goes far beyond the credit she has been given in the history of the country.

A Groundbreaking
Journalist

Pamela Newkirk

Both in Europe and the United States, newspapers and
other forums for journalistic writing proliferated during
the nineteenth century. The Industrial Revolution had
served both to facilitate mass production of newspapers and
to create more leisure time for middle-class readers to pe-
ruse them. Although women composed a good segment of
the reading public, female journalists were the exception
rather than the rule. A black woman journalist such as Ida
B. Wells-Barnett was by definition unusual, especially
when she consistently reported on serious social and political matters such as racial discrimination and the terrible
epidemic of lynching. The following selection by Pamela
Newkirk focuses on Wells-Barnett's life in terms of her remarkable achievements in journalism. Newkirk stresses
how Wells-Barnett used the power of the press to decry
racial injustice, a quest that occupied her throughout her
adult life. Newkirk is an associate professor of journalism
and mass communication at New York University.

❦   ❦   ❦

Pamela Newkirk, "Journalism as a Weapon Against Racial Bigotry," *Media Studies
Journal*, vol. 14, Spring/Summer 2000. Copyright © 2000 by *Media Studies Journal*. Reproduced by permission.

O n May 4, 1884, more than 70 years before Rosa Parks fueled the civil rights movement by refusing to give up her seat on a bus to a white man, 22-year-old Ida B. Wells spurned a segregated train car to sit in the ladies' coach. After she was forcefully removed from the coach, she exited the train, hired an attorney and sued the Chesapeake & Ohio Railroad Company on the grounds that blacks were relegated to the smoking car when the law called for separate and equal public accommodations. A court awarded her $500 in damages.

Journalism as a Weapon

"Darky Damsel Gets Damages," reported the *Memphis Daily Appeal* on December 25, 1884. While the state supreme court reversed the circuit court ruling in 1887, the experience helped launch the career of a fearless journalist who unflinchingly put her livelihood and life on the line to confront racial injustice. After writing about her legal battle in a religious newsweekly, *Living Way*, Wells would for another four decades use journalism as a weapon against the virulent racial bigotry sweeping the South.

In 1889 Wells' *Living Way* columns under the pen name Iola were nationally circulated in black newspapers. That year she was invited to write for *Free Speech and Headlight*, which was co-owned by the pastor of Tennessee's largest Baptist church. Wells insisted on coming on board at *Free Speech and Headlight* as an equal partner. She became editor and one-third owner of the paper while maintaining her job as a Memphis public school teacher. For two years, she operated on dual fronts without incident. But in 1891, she turned her critical pen toward inferior conditions in the city's black public schools. The article cost her the coveted teaching job she had held for seven years.

She later wrote that she had tried to avoid losing her job by asking Rev. F. Nightingale, part owner and sales manager of the paper, to sign his name to the critical article. "I was still teaching and I wanted to hold my position," Wells wrote in her autobiography. When he refused, it was published unsigned, leading many to rightly assume she had written it.

Of her dismissal, she wrote, "Of course I had rather feared that might be the result; but I had taken a chance in the interest of the children of our race and had lost out. The worst part of the experience was the lack of appreciation shown by the parents. They simply couldn't understand why one would risk a good job, even for their children. . . . But I thought it was right to strike a blow against a glaring evil and I did not regret it."

The "Princess of the Press"

The loss of her job allowed Wells to turn her full attention to journalism. She was already known in black circles throughout the country as "Princess of the Press" for her contributions to many of the nation's leading black newspapers. The *New York Age*, the respected black weekly, regularly reprinted her *Free Speech* articles. Being an outspoken woman in a male-dominated profession only served to bolster her celebrity.

"She has become famous as one of the few women who handle a goose quill with diamond point as easily as any man in newspaper work," wrote T. Thomas Fortune, the legendary editor of the *New York Age*. "If Iola were a man she would be a humming independent in politics. She has plenty of nerve and is as sharp as a steel trap." Given the precarious status of blacks in the South during that era, when blacks were openly attacked by mobs, her outspokenness against the widespread disenfranchisement and persecution of blacks would have been noteworthy even for a man.

Investigating Lynching

This was particularly so in 1892, when she began high-lighting the widespread lynching of black men through-out the South, which had become a routine and publicly sanctioned form of justice. Her interest was piqued by the lynching of three prominent Memphis-area busi-nessmen who managed a store in a heavily populated community. The men, Thomas Moss, Calvin McDow-ell and Henry Steward, had been charged, by a compet-ing white grocery store owner, with conspiracy and in-dicted. The indictment triggered protests in Memphis' black community, and after four days of unrest, Moss, McDowell and Steward were charged with inciting a riot and thrown in jail. They were then taken from the county jail, shot and hanged, with graphic details of their lynching recounted in the daily newspaper. It was reported that Moss had begged for his life and that Mc-Dowell, whose fingers were shot off, had tried to grab the gun. For Wells, the incident both underscored the complicity of whites—in the government and in the press—in mob violence against blacks and debunked the prevailing myth that black men were lynched for raping white women.

In her editorial in *Free Speech*, Wells expressed out-rage that "the city of Memphis has demonstrated that neither character nor standing avails the Negro if he dares to protect himself against the white man or be-come his rival." She implored blacks to "save our money and leave a town which will neither protect our lives and property, nor give us a fair trial in the courts, when accused by white persons." She also urged blacks to continue a boycott of the streetcars in protest of the brutal murders.

She began to investigate the lynching of other black men accused of rape, including one reported in an As-sociated Press dispatch from Tunica County in Mississippi. "The big burly brute was lynched because he had raped the seven-year-old daughter of the sheriff," said the report. Wells set out for Tunica County, where she learned that the sheriff's daughter was a grown woman who had been found by her father in the black man's cabin. In another case, the victim's mother told her that her son had responded to the advances of the young mistress of the house and was lynched once their romance was discovered. Incidents such as these prompted her to write her now famous editorial published in *Free Speech* on May 21, 1892. In it, she questioned the purity of white women that was typically held up to justify the lynching of black men.

An Address to President McKinley on Lynching

In 1898 Ida B. Wells-Barnett, representing a Chicago delegation, gave an address to President William McKinley concerning the lynching of a black postmaster in South Carolina. Her speech, excerpted here, calls on the president to seek justice against the perpetrators, provide compensation for his surviving family, and push for national antilynching legislation.

Mr. President, the colored citizens of this country in general, and Chicago in particular, desire to respectfully urge that some action be taken by you as chief magistrate of this great nation, first for the apprehension and punishment of the lynchers of Postmaster Baker, of Lake City, S.C.; second, we ask indemnity for the widow and children, both for the murder of the husband and father, and for injuries sustained by themselves; third, we most earnestly desire that national legislation be enacted for the suppression of the national crime of lynching.

For nearly twenty years lynching crimes, which stand

"Nobody in this section of the country believes the old thread-bare lie that Negro men rape white women," wrote Wells. "If Southern white men are not careful they will over-reach themselves and public sentiment will have a reaction; a conclusion will then be reached which will be very damaging to the moral reputation of their women."

Backlash from the White Press

The editorial sparked angry calls for revenge in the daily newspapers. "Patience under such circumstances is not a virtue," said the editorial in *The Evening Scimitar* of Memphis, Tennessee, on May 25, 1892. "If the

side by side with Armenian and Cuban outrages, have been committed and permitted by this Christian nation. Nowhere in the civilized world save the United States of America do men, possessing all civil and political power, go out in bands of 50 and 5,000 to hunt down, shoot, hang or burn to death a single individual, unarmed and absolutely powerless. Statistics show that nearly 10,000 American citizens have been lynched in the past 20 years. To our appeals for justice the stereotyped reply has been that the government could not interfere in a state matter. Postmaster Baker's case was a federal matter, pure and simple. He died at his post of duty in defense of his country's honor, as truly as did ever a soldier on the field of battle. We refuse to believe this country, so powerful to defend its citizens abroad, is unable to protect its citizens at home. Italy and China have been indemnified by this government for the lynching of their citizens. We ask that the government do as much for its own.

Herbert Aptheker, ed., *A Documentary History of the Negro People in the United States*, vol. 2. New York: Citadel, 1970, p. 798.

negroes themselves do not apply the remedy without delay it will be the duty of those whom he has attacked to tie the wretch who utters these calumnies to a stake at the intersection of Main and Madison Sts., brand him in the forehead with a hot iron and perform upon him a surgical operation with a pair of tailor's shears." Given the male-dominated world of journalism at the time, the writer had little reason to suspect that the editorial had been written by a woman.

The same day, the city's *Daily Commercial* also called for revenge. "The fact that a black scoundrel is allowed to live and utter such loathsome and repulsive calumnies is a volume of evidence as to the wonderful patience of Southern whites. But we have had enough of it. There are some things that the Southern white will not tolerate, and the obscene intimations of the foregoing have brought the writer to the outermost limit of public patience. We hope we have said enough."

While Wells was en route to Philadelphia to attend the African Methodist Episcopal Church's general conference, the office of *Free Speech* was destroyed and its business manager, J.L. Fleming, was run out of town. Wells learned of the mob attack while meeting in New Jersey with Fortune, who showed her an account of the incident in the *New York Sun*. The article said that a group of leading citizens, acting on the *Commercial Appeal* editorial, had destroyed the type and furnishings in the *Free Speech* office and left a note warning that anyone who tried to publish the paper would be killed.

"Although I had been warned repeatedly by my own people that something would happen if I did not cease harping on the lynching of three months before, I had expected the happening to come when I was at home," Wells wrote in her autobiography. "I had bought a pistol the first thing after Tom Moss was lynched, because I expected some cowardly retaliation from the lynchers.

I felt that one had better die fighting against injustice than to die like a dog or a rat in a trap."

Broadening the Crusade

Urged by friends not to return to Memphis, Wells decided to stay in New York where she joined the staff of the *New York Age*. She was also given one-quarter interest in exchange for her *Free Speech* subscription list. "They had destroyed my paper, in which every dollar I had in the world was invested. They had made me an exile and threatened my life for hinting at the truth. I felt that I owed it to myself and my race to tell the whole truth," she would say later.

At the *Age*, Wells continued her aggressive crusade against lynching. She published a pamphlet, *Southern Horrors: Lynch Law in All Its Phases* which documented the epidemic throughout the South. It was the first time the atrocity against blacks had been thoroughly documented and the complicity of the white establishment highlighted. In many communities, white citizens would attend the public lynching of blacks—who were often set ablaze—for amusement. Such episodes were gleefully reported in the press. Wells was particularly horrified by a lynching in Paris, Texas, in February 1893 in which schoolchildren were given a holiday to see a murder suspect burned alive after being tortured for hours with red-hot irons.

"Brave woman! You have done your people and mine a service which can neither be weighed nor measured," wrote Frederick Douglass in a letter to Wells dated October 25, 1892, which she reprinted in her pamphlet on lynching, *Southern Horrors*. The documentation of lynching along with her national speaking tours in the United States drew international attention. She accepted an invitation to travel to England, Scotland and Wales in 1893 to publicize both the barbaric practice and the failure of prominent white Americans to condemn it. She riveted her European audiences with stories of American barbarity, and her speeches were widely reported on and editorialized. She was particularly critical of the American mainstream press, which was, at best, mute on the issue. "The pulpit and the press of our own country remains silent on these continued outrages and the voice of my race thus tortured and outraged is stifled or ignored wherever it is lifted in America in a demand for justice," she wrote in a letter to the editor published in the *Daily Post* in Birmingham, England, on May 16, 1893.

Wells' critique of the press earned her public enemies. The president of the Missouri Press Association, in a letter published in a local newspaper, denounced Wells and all black women who, he said, had "no sense of virtue and [were] altogether without character."

Other Journalistic Accomplishments

While best known for her exposés on lynching, Wells wrote about a wide range of issues affecting African Americans. In 1893, in collaboration with Frederick Douglass, Ferdinand Barnett (whom she later married) and I. Garland Penn, they produced *The Reason Why the Colored American Is Not in the World's Columbian Exposition*. The 81-page booklet condemned the exclusion of black Americans in the Chicago World's Fair. In the preface she wrote:

> The exhibit of the progress made by a race in 25 years of freedom as against 250 years of slavery would have been the greatest tribute to the greatness and progressiveness of American institutions which could have been shown to the world. The colored people of this great Republic number eight millions—more than one-tenth of the whole population of the United States. They were among the earliest settlers of the continent, landing at Jamestown, Virginia, in

1619 in a slave ship, before the Puritans, who landed at Plymouth in 1620. They have contributed a large share to American prosperity and civilization. The labor of one-half of this country has always been, and is still being done by them. . . . The wealth created by their industry has afforded to the white people of this country the leisure essential to their great progress in education, art, science, industry and invention.

In 1894 she returned to England, where for six months she lectured while regularly writing articles published in the newspaper the *Chicago Inter-Ocean*. She returned to the United States in July 1894. The following year she settled in Chicago and published *A Red Record: Tabulated Statistics and Alleged Causes of Lynchings in the United States, 1892–1893–1894*. She wrote:

It becomes a painful duty of the Negro to reproduce a record which shows that a large portion of the American people avow anarchy, condone murder and defy the contempt of civilization. These pages are written in no spirit of vindictiveness, for all who give the subject [of lynching] consideration must concede that far too serious is the condition of that civilized government in which the spirit of unrestrained outlawry constantly increases in violence, and casts it blight over a continually growing area of territory. . . . During the year 1894, there were 132 persons executed in the United States by due form of law, while in the same year, 197 persons were put to death by mobs who gave the victims no opportunity to make a lawful defense. No comment need be made upon a condition of public sentiment responsible for such alarming results.

The *Red Record* provided not only statistics, most gathered through mainstream press accounts, but also a detailed overview of the history of lynching since the Emancipation Proclamation.

Wells married Ferdinand L. Barnett in 1895. Barnett, a lawyer, founded *The Conservator*, the first black newspaper in Chicago. The couple had three children, but Wells continued her newspaper work and anti-lynching crusade. She would later write for the nation's major black weeklies, most notably the *Chicago Defender*, for which she covered the race riots in Springfield, Illinois; Elaine, Arkansas; and East St. Louis, Illinois, the latter in which 150 blacks were killed in July of 1917. Her dispatches included interviews from scenes of violence, from the looted homes of blacks and from the municipal lodgings where blacks were driven by angry white mobs.

In the preface to her autobiography, Wells, who died in 1931 at the age of 68, maintained her fierce racial pride. She stressed the importance of blacks recording their own history, noting that the major accomplishments of blacks during Reconstruction—when blacks served in such high positions as lieutenant governor, governor and U.S. senator—were "buried in oblivion. . . . [O]nly the southern white man's misrepresentations are in the public libraries and college textbooks of the land. The black men who made the history of that day were too modest to write of it, or did not realize the importance of the written word to their posterity."

It is something that could never be said of Wells-Barnett, who seemed always to realize the power—and the danger—of the written word.

Burned Alive

Ida B. Wells-Barnett

Although lynch mobs favored hanging, it was not the sole method employed by racist vigilantes to victimize blacks. In her crusade against lynching, Ida B. Wells-Barnett called attention to all forms of mob-driven murder, including lynching by fire. In the following selection from her 1900 pamphlet "Mob Rule in New Orleans," Wells-Barnett enumerates several instances in which black men were burned alive by racist mobs. She provides often gruesome detail as part of her overall journalistic strategy, which was to shock and shame her readers with evidence of horrific barbarity perpetuated by a supposedly "civilized" white populace. Wells-Barnett condemns not only the mobs that tortured and killed their black victims but also the thousands of men, women, and even children who stood by and watched in approval.

☙ ☙ ☙

Not only has life been taken by mobs in the past twenty years, but the ordinary procedure of hanging and shooting have been improved upon during the past ten years. Fifteen human beings have been burned to death in the different parts of the country by mobs. Men,

Ida B. Wells-Barnett, *On Lynchings*. Salem, NH: Ayer, 1991.

women and children have gone to see the sight, and all have approved the barbarous deeds done in the high light of the civilization and Christianity of this country.

Celebrating Murder

In 1891 Ed Coy was burned to death in Texarkana, Ark. He was charged with assaulting a white woman, and after the mob had securely tied him to a tree, the men and boys amused themselves for some time sticking knives into Coy's body and slicing off pieces of flesh. When they had amused themselves sufficiently, they poured coal oil over him and the women in the case set fire to him. It is said that fifteen thousand people stood by and saw him burned. This was on a Sunday night, and press reports told how the people looked on while the Negro burned to death.

Feb. 1st, 1893, Henry Smith was burned to death in Paris, Texas. The entire county joined in that exhibition. The district attorney himself went for the prisoner and turned him over to the mob. He was placed upon a float and drawn by four white horses through the principal streets of the city. Men, women and children stood at their doors and waved their handkerchiefs and cheered the echoes. They knew that the man was to be burned to death because the newspaper had declared for three days previous that this would be so. Excursions were run by all the railroads, and the mayor of the town gave the children a holiday so that they might see the sight. Henry Smith was charged with having assaulted and murdered a little white girl He was an imbecile, and while he had killed the child, there was no proof that he had criminally assaulted. He was tied to a stake on a platform which had been built ten feet high, so that everybody might see the sight. The father and brother and uncle of the little white girl that had been murdered was upon that platform about fifty minutes entertaining the crowd of ten thousand persons by burning the victim's flesh with red-hot irons. Their own newspapers told how they burned his eyes out and ran the red-hot iron down his throat, cooking his tongue, and how the crowd cheered with delight. At last, having declared themselves satisfied, coal oil was poured over him and he was burned to death, and the mob fought over the ashes for bones and pieces of his clothes.

Innocent Victims

July 7th, 1893, in Bardwell, Ky., C.J. Miner was burned to ashes. Since his death this man has been found to be absolutely innocent of the murder of the two white girls with which he was charged. But the mob would wait for no justification. They insisted that, as they were not sure he was the right man, they would compromise the matter by hanging him instead of burning. Not to be outdone, they took the body down and made a huge bonfire out of it.

July 22d, 1893, at Memphis, Tenn., the body of Lee Walker was dragged through the street and burned before the court house. Walker had frightened some girls in a wagon along a country road by asking them to let him ride in their wagon. They cried out; some men working in a field nearby said it was an attempt of assault, and of course began to look for their prey. There was never any charge of rape; the women only declared that he attempted an assault. After he was apprehended and put in jail and perfectly helpless, the mob dragged him out, shot him, cut him, beat him with sticks, built a fire and burned the legs off, then took the trunk of the body down and dragged further up the street, and at last burned it before the court house.

Sept. 20th, 1893, at Roanoke, Va., the body of a Negro who had quarreled with a white woman was burned in the presence of several thousand persons. These people also wreaked their vengeance upon this helpless victim of the mob's wrath by sticking knives into him, kicking him and beating him with stones and otherwise mutilating him before life was extinct.

Senseless Violence

June 10th, 1898, at Knoxville, Ark., James Perry was shut up in a cabin because he had smallpox and burned to death. He had been quarantined in this cabin when it was declared that he had this disease and the doctor sent for. When the physician arrived he found only a few smoldering embers. Upon inquiry some railroad hands were working nearby revealed the fact that they had fastened the door of the cabin and set fire to the cabin and burned man and hut together.

Ida B. Wells-Barnett

Feb. 22d, 1898, at Lake City, S.C., Postmaster Baker and his infant child were burned to death by a mob that had set fire to his house. Mr. Baker's crime was that he had refused to give up the postoffice, to which he had been appointed by the National Government. The mob had tried to drive him away by persecution and intimidation. Finding that all else had failed, they went to his home in the dead of night and set fire to his house, and as the family rushed forth they were greeted by a volley of bullets. The father and his baby were shot through the open door and wounded so badly that they fell back in the fire and were burned to death. The remainder of the family, consisting of the wife and five children, escaped with their lives from the burning house, but all of them were shot, one of the number made a cripple for life.

Jan. 7th, 1898, two Indians were tied to a tree at Maud Postoffice, Indian Territory, and burned to death by a white mob. They were charged with murdering a white woman. There was no proof of their guilt except the unsupported word of the mob. Yet they were tied to a tree and slowly roasted to death. Their names were Lewis McGeesy and Hond Martin. Since that time these boys have been found to be absolutely innocent of the charge. Of course that discovery is too late to be of any benefit to them, but because they were Indians the Indian Commissioner demanded and received from the United States Government an indemnity of $13,000.

Mob Injustice in Georgia

April 23d, 1899, at Palmetto, Ga., Sam Hose was burned alive in the presence of a throng, on Sunday afternoon.

He was charged with killing a man named Cranford, his employer, which he admitted he did because his employer was about to shoot him. To the fact of killing the employer was added the absolutely false charge that Hose assaulted the wife. Hose was arrested and no trial was given him. According to the code of reasoning of the mob, none was needed. A white man had been killed and a white woman was said to have been assaulted. That was enough. When Hose was found he had to die.

The *Atlanta Constitution*, in speaking of the murder of Cranford, said that the Negro who was suspected would be burned alive. Not only this, but it offered a $500 reward for his capture. After he had been apprehended, it was publicly announced that he would be burned alive. Excursion trains were run and bulletins were put up in the small towns. The Governor of Georgia was in Atlanta while excursion trains were being made up to take visitors to the burning. Many fair ladies drove out in their carriages on Sunday afternoon to witness the torture and burning of a human being. Hose's ears were cut off, then his toes and fingers, and passed round to the crowd. His eyes were put out, his tongue torn out and flesh cut in strips by knives. Finally they poured coal oil on him and burned him to death. They dragged his half-consumed trunk out of the flames, cut it open, extracted his heart and liver, and sold slices for ten cents each for souvenirs, all of which was published most promptly in the daily papers of Georgia and boasted over by the people of that section.

No Proof of Guilt

Oct. 19th, 1889, at Canton, Miss., Joseph Leflore was burned to death. A house had been entered and its occupants murdered during the absence of the husband and father. When the discovery was made, it was immediately supposed that the crime was the work of a Negro, and the motive that of assaulting white women.

Bloodhounds were procured and they made a round of the village and discovered only one colored man absent from his home. This was taken to be proof sufficient that he was the perpetrator of the deed. When he returned home he was apprehended, taken into the yard of the house that had been burned down, tied to a stake, and was slowly roasted to death.

Dec. 6th, 1899, at Maysville, Ky., Wm. Coleman also was burned to death. He was slowly roasted, first one foot and then the other, and dragged out of the fire so that the torture might be prolonged. All of this without a shadow of proof or scintilla of evidence that the man had committed the crime.

Thus have the mobs of this country taken the lives of their victims within the last ten years. In every single instance except one these burnings were witnessed by from two thousand to fifteen thousand people, and no one person in all these crowds throughout the country had the courage to raise his voice and speak out against the awful barbarism of burning human beings to death.

Men and women of America, are you proud of this record which the Anglo-Saxon race has made for itself? Your silence seems to say that you are. Your silence encourages a continuance of this sort of Horror. Only by earnest, active, united endeavor to arouse public sentiment can we hope to put a stop to these demonstrations of American barbarism.

CHAPTER

2

Winnie Mandela

Winnie Mandela's Troubled Life

Martin Meredith

Because Winnie Mandela has been a polarizing figure throughout her public life, her detractors are as numerous as her admirers. The following profile by Martin Meredith is not entirely unsympathetic, but the author stresses nonetheless Mandela's many legal and political problems. Meredith suggests that Winnie Mandela the activist may have used her imprisoned husband's reputation to further her own considerable political ambitions. Meredith, the author of several books on African politics and history (including a biography of Nelson Mandela), seems to regard Winnie as more a ruthless opportunist than an authentic coleader with her ex-husband of the antiapartheid movement in South Africa.

🐾 🐾 🐾

She's revered by thousands in the townships still. Will dark stories from the past halt Mrs Mandela's march towards power?

Winnie Mandela has survived so many scandals dur-

Martin Meredith, "The Trouble with Winnie," *New Statesman*, vol. 126, September 26, 1997, p. 44. Copyright © 1997 by New Statesman, Ltd. Reproduced by permission.

ing the last ten years that she has gained a reputation for being untouchable. The list of allegations made against her include murder, assault and abduction, dating back to the time during the late 1980s when her personal bodyguard, the Mandela United Football Club, became notorious for what local black leaders described as "a reign of terror" in Soweto. Several of Winnie's former associates are serving prison sentences; one of them alone was convicted of nine murders. But the only penalty Winnie has so far paid for her role as head of the football club is a 15,000 Rand fine for ordering the kidnapping of a 14-year-old boy, Stompie Moeketsi, who was subsequently murdered by the club's "coach".

Since that time Winnie has been free to pursue her relentless drive for high office. Despite her divorce from Nelson Mandela [in 1996] and her ignominious dismissal as a junior minister from his government the year before, she has regained the initiative by being nominated as a candidate in the election for the post of deputy president of the ruling African National Congress to be held at a party congress in December. If she wins that contest she would become a leading contender for the job of deputy president of South Africa in the post-Mandela era in 1999 and thus only a heartbeat away from the presidency itself.

New Questions About Old Scandals

But just when the way ahead seemed clear Winnie has been beset by ghosts from the past. A new spate of allegations about her activities in the 1980s has surfaced as a result of the work of the Truth and Reconciliation Commission, set up by President Mandela to investigate and account for a range of crimes during the apartheid era. Hoping to gain an amnesty for their own involvement in club activities, witnesses have pointed the finger at Winnie. She has duly been summoned to appear before closed hearings of the commission to face cross-examination about her alleged links to 18 crimes, including eight murders. One report described the subpoena given to her as reading like "a script for a horror movie".

One of Winnie's accusers is the football team's coach, Jerry Richardson, a suspected police informer who habitually referred to Winnie as "Mummy" and who is serving a life sentence for Stompie's murder. At his trial in 1990 Richardson denied killing Stompie and he also denied that Winnie had been present when Stompie and three other kidnap victims were brought to her house in Soweto in December 1988 and subjected to prolonged beating. Now Richardson admits to the murder and insists that Winnie participated in the beatings. "I lied to save Winnie Mandela," he told a newspaper reporter in prison. In a television interview earlier this month [1997] he claimed he had killed Stompie "under instructions from Mrs Mandela".

During Winnie's 1991 trial for the kidnapping and assault of Stompie, two of the surviving kidnap victims described in graphic detail how Winnie had led the assaults, punching and slapping them, before other members of the football club joined in. In her defence Winnie produced an alibi claiming that she had been on a visit to Brandfort, 200 miles away, at the time. Two of her co-defendants supported her claim. Even though the police possessed documentary evidence to show that Winnie was in Soweto and not in Brandfort, it was never produced in court. Now the two co-defendants have admitted they lied to protect Winnie.

More Mysterious Deaths
But the fate of Stompie is the least of Winnie's troubles. She has also been linked to the murder of her close

friend Dr Abu-Baker Asvat, a popular Indian doctor who had been called to her house to examine Stompie shortly before his death and who was therefore a key witness. Asvat was murdered in his surgery in Soweto four weeks later, in January 1989, by two Zulu youths, one of whom has now sought from prison an amnesty, claiming that he carried out the killing on instructions from Mrs Mandela.

Winnie is also being questioned about the disappearance and death of two young activists, Lolo Sono and Siboniso Tshabalala, in November 1988. According to Sono's father, he last saw Lolo battered and bleeding in the back of Winnie's minibus. Winnie told him that Lolo was a "sell-out". The father pleaded with Winnie to let the youth go. But Winnie refused and drove off. Richardson has implicated Winnie in the murder of both Sono and his friend Tshabalala, who disappeared at the same time.

Another murder that Winnie ordered, according to Richardson, was that of Kuki Zwane, a close friend of her daughter Zindzi. In his television interview Richardson admitted that he had carried out the killing. "The fact that Kuki Zwane was killed is because Mrs Mandela handed down a task and said: 'Richardson, Kuki Zwane is disturbing me, she's bothering me'," he said.

Winnie Remains Defiant

Winnie's response has been to deny everything and to assert that it is all part of a campaign by her political enemies to destroy her reputation before the ANC Congress in December—"a last vicious attempt to remove me from the political arena". She predicts: "They have tried so hard for decades and failed. This time they will fail for ever."

The outcome is unclear. Several key witnesses are themselves convicted criminals with records of perjury.

The evidence of one key witness, Katiza Cebekhulu, who is in hiding in exile under the protection of the former British MP Emma Nicholson, has already been dismissed by the national police commissioner, George Fivaz, as "unreliable". A significant body of opinion in South Africa holds that the accusations against Winnie are no more than propaganda.

Yet even today, nearly ten years after the demise of Mandela United, there are dozens of witnesses and family members living in Soweto who tremble when recalling its brutal existence and who are still too frightened to speak openly. The reality is that Winnie's football club was an evil mess, which no one has yet been willing to confront.

A Naive and Rebellious Young Woman

When Nelson Mandela began his prison sentence in 1962 he knew how difficult life would be for Winnie without him. In the treacherous world of South African politics she was a novice, naive and gullible, with a headstrong and impetuous temperament likely to lead her into trouble, and easy prey for the security police. In a letter written to her on the eve of his imprisonment he had tried to offer her encouragement for the long and lonely road she faced, urging her to act with fortitude and dignity and warning of the traps that would be set for her. It was a letter that Winnie cherished, reading it time and again until it was seized by security police during one of their periodic raids on her house in Soweto.

Their marriage had been lived in brief fragments. When they first met in 1957 Mandela was on trial for treason, a charge that carried the death penalty; his law practice was falling apart; he was in serious financial difficulty; his first marriage had disintegrated and he rarely had enough time to see his three children. But he was captivated by Winnie's beauty and determined to marry her. At their wedding reception in 1958 Winnie's father warned: "This marriage will be no bed of roses."

Winnie was 23 years old at the time, 16 years younger than Mandela, a qualified social worker well regarded for her enthusiastic nature and willingness to help others. But her childhood had been marked by rebelliousness, harsh discipline and family discord. She was often embroiled in fights and gained a reputation among other children as a bully. As a student she earned herself nicknames on the sports field such as "The Amazon Queen" and "Lady Tarzan". "I solved problems the simple way, using physical force, as I had done way back in my childhood days," she once explained.

Her interest in politics was negligible; she took a far greater interest in clothes. Mandela never confided in Winnie. She was simply told what to do. When, in 1961, he decided to go underground, Winnie was given no forewarning. He merely arrived back home one day and said: "Darling, just pack some of my clothes in a suitcase with my toiletries. I will be going away for a long time."

Activism and Persecution

Once Mandela was in prison, however, Winnie became more ambitious. She saw herself as Mandela's heir, capable of acting on his behalf. Towards other activists she adopted a superior manner, making herself unpopular with them. She also had a propensity for becoming involved with shady characters, including police informers "Winnie always acted on her own," Rusty Bernstein, one of Mandela's close colleagues, recalled. "She wouldn't co-operate with anyone. She refused to take advice. She was an individual piece of militancy."

The security police persecuted her endlessly. In 1969 police interrogators questioned her for five days and nights until she broke, confessing to everything they de-

manded, and then despatched her to solitary confine-
ment for 18 months, where she was constantly taunted
by white warders and hovered at times on the borders of
insanity. Recalling the experience 20 years later, she remarked: "It is in fact what changed me; what brutalised
me so much that I knew what it is to hate."

How much Winnie changed became evident during
the late 1980s when many of South Africa's black townships were engulfed in the turmoil of anti-apartheid re-
volt and government repression. The bodyguard that
Winnie formed soon began operating as a vigilante
group, feared throughout Soweto. A report sent to the
ANC's leader in exile, Oliver Tambo, warned that
Winnie was out of control, but Tambo could provide
no solution. Local black leaders formed a crisis committee, but felt powerless to confront Winnie. The police were no longer willing to be seen persecuting her
and witnesses were reluctant to come forward; the government, on the brink of seeking ways to open negoti-
ations for a political settlement in South Africa, wanted
no new embarrassment over Winnie to impede it. She
thus enjoyed a kind of immunity, which not only in-
duced greater fear of her in the community but increased her own sense of power.

Only murmurs of Winnie's activities reached Mandela in prison. Friends and lawyers visiting him were
careful not to draw too much attention to her conduct
or her heavy drinking, to avoid unduly alarming him.
For years Mandela had been racked by feelings of guilt
and frustration about the persistent harassment of his
wife at the hands of the security police. He was also in
poor health, recovering from tuberculosis, well aware of
Winnie's wayward nature but convinced that she had
committed no more than "errors of judgment" in becoming involved with rough elements in Soweto. The
brief glimpses of Winnie that he had enjoyed during

prison visits over the years had given him little under-standing of her changed character. In Mandela's com-pany Winnie was warm and vivacious, dressed to dazzle.

Winnie's Loyalists

Released from prison, Mandela held fast to his belief in Winnie's innocence. At the time of her trial in 1991 he remarked: "One of the aims of this case is to destroy the image of Comrade Winnie, and myself, and the ANC."

Much the same view is taken today by Winnie's sup-porters.

Since then Winnie has cultivated a mass following in the squatter communities of South Africa, presenting herself as the champion of the poor and downtrodden, and adopting radical positions that appeal to the dis-gruntled. Even when she was a minister in Mandela's government she became increasingly critical of the slow pace of reform. "Nothing has changed," she said, shortly before getting the sack. "In fact your struggle seems much worse than before, when the fight was against the Boers."

The ground swell of disillusion with Mandela's gov-ernment now provides fertile territory on which to make her populist pitch. It is the massed ranks of the poor, she believes, that will eventually carry her to power. And no one there cares much about what hap-pened ten years ago during the apartheid regime.

The Soweto Uprising

Winnie Mandela

On June 16, 1976, some thirty thousand young black students in Soweto, South Africa, marched through the streets to protest the government mandate that Afrikaans be the language of classroom instruction in secondary schools. When police confronted the youthful protesters, violence erupted, leaving a thirteen-year-old boy, Hector Peterson, dead from a gunshot wound. Riots erupted in black South African communities. By the time the unrest was quelled, at least six hundred were dead and fifteen hundred were wounded, the majority of the casualties students. In the following selection excerpted from her 1984 autobiography, Winnie Mandela offers a firsthand account of the Soweto uprising and its bloody consequences.

🐝 🐝 🐝

In June 1976 the anger of young blacks in South Africa against the injustices of the regime had reached boiling point.

Twenty thousand children marched with slogans attacking Bantu Education and demanding the release of

Winnie Mandela, *Part of My Soul Went with Him*, edited by Anne Benjamin. New York: W.W. Norton, 1984. Copyright © 1984 by Rowohlt Taschenbuch Verlag GmbH, Reinbek bei Hamburg. Reproduced by permission of the publisher.

[Nelson] Mandela, [human rights activist Walter] Sisulu, and other political prisoners. The lessons of 1976 are there for anybody to see: here were children who ought to think of Mandela as a myth, who ought to think of him as somebody of the past. But they were singing about our leaders on Robben Island. They recognized a leadership that has been incarcerated for nearly twenty years.

The Rage of Children

June 1976, known as the 'uprising of Soweto', was a spontaneous flare-up of the country. No one organized it. The eruption on 16 June was an escalation of what had been simmering for weeks already. In May there had been open talk amongst the kids of taking action on the issue of Afrikaans in their schools: they had long been angry about this.

I was there among them, I saw what happened. The children picked up stones, they used dustbin lids as shields and marched towards machine guns. It's not that they don't know that the white man is heavily armed; they marched against heavy machine gun fire. You could smell gunfire everywhere. Children were dying in the street, and as they were dying, the others marched forward, facing guns. No one has ever underestimated the power of the enemy. We know that he is armed to the teeth. But the determination, the thirst for freedom in children's hearts, was such that they were prepared to face those machine guns with stones. That is what happens when you hunger for freedom, when you want to break those chains of oppression. Nothing else seems to matter.

Parents Organize

We couldn't stop our children. We couldn't keep them off the streets. On 17 June—one day after hundreds of them had been shot in Soweto, we established the Black Parents Association (BPA).

We found ourselves in the middle of the conflict. The students demanded that we negotiate with Kruger, then Minister of Police. It was a mandate from the students who told us: 'If you want us to stop, go and tell Kruger our grievances.'

I was actually happy that Kruger refused to see us; he couldn't have done anything better. I was hoping he would refuse because it would have put our credibility at stake. Of course we wanted the bloodshed to stop, we didn't believe that our students should be cannon fodder; on the other hand, we had their mandate to negotiate. They would have felt we had let them down by not going. In that emotional atmosphere you could not argue. So Kruger saved us a lot by refusing.

In the Black Parents Association we had people from all schools of thought—religious leaders, social workers, different views from ours. I worked closely with Dr Motlana, Dr Mathlare and Bishop Buthelezi, our chairman.

In the BPA the children saw a mouthpiece, and the system automatically recognized it as their mouthpiece, although we were more active as a welfare organization. We raised money and organized mass burials, since hundreds of families didn't have any funds. Families had to be fed; there were orphans, who sometimes had only a grandmother left, who had to be taken care of. It was most painful when the authorities impounded something like R194,000 which had been donated for the victims.

The Authorities' Accusation

The only time we ever saw any authority on the other side was when we went to Protea police station to plead that they should refrain from shooting at demonstrating children. As we entered, this Major Visser said something like this: 'You organized the riots, and now that they are

out of control, you come to us. You know that you, Winnie Mandela, are entirely responsible for this.' There was
the usual flare-up. I don't think Bishop Buthelezi had ever
seen anything like that in his life. I wanted to restrain myself because of him but it was difficult.

We could not direct the students' activities, that was
not our duty. But when we launched the BPA in May, I
had addressed the Afrikaans issue: 'We must not let the
children fight their battle for us, they must have our
support,' I said. 'What the children learn in school is
also our responsibility. If we let them down now, they
will spit on our graves one day.'

The system maintained that I was manipulating and
directing the struggle of the children. The whole reason behind all this was to discredit one politically, to
show that the [African National Congress] spearheaded
the uprising and that this was the quality of leadership
that was involved. The same old story of agitators!

An Interview with Winnie Mandela

Tanu T. Henry

The following selection is excerpted from one of Winnie Mandela's most recent interviews, conducted in March 2003, shortly before her April fraud trial for which she was convicted. Interviewer Tanu T. Henry, a writer for *Africana* magazine, asks Mandela about her views on the then-pending U.S. invasion of Iraq as well as the current state of South African politics. Although Mandela requested that she not be asked about the criminal trial that was awaiting her, she treats all other topics with characteristic candor, refusing to express regrets over the past or to withdraw from what she clearly sees as the unfinished struggle in South Africa for a just and equitable society.

❧ ❧ ❧

In the 1980s, Winnie Mandela's emotional fire and un-blinking courage attracted global sympathy to the cause and ordeal of Nelson Mandela, her then-imprisoned then-husband. Her courage helped draw attention to the plight of all black South Africans during the country's apartheid regime. Since then, though, she's faced an increasingly critical reception as she bumbled through a thicket of scandals, a highly-publicized divorce, and finally her alleged involvement in the 1989 murder of a 14-year-old Soweto youth activist, Stompie Seipei. Most recently, she's been charged with embezzling some $100,000 from the African National Congress, her former husband's political party. She denies both charges.

At 68, Mandela looks older than she did during the divestment era, but she's still stunning. She seemed calmer than before, as if she's mostly forged her passion into a more temperate commitment to her various causes. Still, like everyone's favorite outrageous aunt, she's capable of the occasional fiery retort and catty sotto voce pronouncement.

As a precondition, I was asked not to inquire about Seipei's murder or the fraud charges. But she did share her thoughts on the African National Congress, President Thabo Mbeki, Nelson Mandela and other global issues like Zimbabwe's land reform program, the pending war with Iraq, South Africa's Truth and Reconciliation Commission and Affirmative Action.

Driving Political Passions

I read that you want to go to Iraq as a human shield. What motivates that decision?

I was misquoted. I said I believe that war in any country belongs to mothers more than it belongs to men. I was suggesting that South Africa send a delegation of women to Saddam Hussein. And I would be honored to lead that delegation. We have that painful history—we have seen thousands of our children perish in the struggle. And at the end of the day, they are not the beneficiaries of any war. South Africa suggested sending a delegation of war experts, nine men, to Iraq and no one ever thought about the mothers who bring this life, who gave birth to Saddam Hussein himself. We are the ones who suffer the loss of these lives in the event of war. I am totally against war. No one wants to see life lost. And one life lost is one too many.

What is your role in the South African government now?

I am the head of the Women's League of the African National Congress, ANC—that is just the women's wing of the ANC. What occupies us is exactly what occupies government. We are engaged in preventive measures to help stem the scourge of HIV. We have passed that stage of just dealing with feminist issues. Women have common experiences, but I am not one of those feminists who believe that there are separate women's issues and separate men's issues. I fought right alongside men during the revolution.

Governance in Postapartheid South Africa

What do you think about Thabo Mbeki? Do you think he's doing enough to create the new, multiracial and democratic South Africa?

Within his capacity he is addressing very difficult issues. You must remember that we come from a very painful past. We cannot undo, just in his term of office, what has been done by the Afrikaners, the ruling white racist regimes of yesteryear. To undo that just in his term will be a miracle.

What about former President Nelson Mandela?

Mandela, too. What they have all done so far is within their own limitations. It is a country that was bled dry by apartheid, ravaged by racism. It is not easy to level those playing fields. It is going to take some time. Some feel that we are not transforming South Africa quickly enough. But we are doing the best we can to address those economic and social inequalities.

What do you think about President Mbeki's view that HIV does not cause AIDS?

I can only speak for myself. I think President Mbeki's

views can best be explained by himself. I believe HIV causes AIDS. I believe in the scientific explanation of AIDS and we have had personal experiences. There are very few families in South Africa that have not experienced a loss of a family member from AIDS. My brother's children have died from AIDS. Politicians should stick to politics and scientists should deal with issues like AIDS.

Britain has criticized South Africa for not taking a firm stance against [Zimbabwe's president] Robert Mugabe's controversial land reform program. Do you think the South African government has been critical enough?

I don't think South Africa should have to monitor its neighbor where there is a democratically elected government. I may have my own personal views, which I wouldn't like to express because I don't want to pretend to be an expert.

What are those views?

In South Africa, the struggle was about land. When we fought as ferociously as we did, we were fighting for our land. Whether Mugabe is fighting for his land in a different manner, I don't know. That is an issue that should be decided by the people of Zimbabwe.

What do you think about the African Union, though? Wouldn't that require, by nature, more interdependence and intervention between countries?

Any attempt to rectify the ills of the continent, any attempt to try and improve on what the Organization of African Unity [OAU] stood for, would be welcomed if it brought about change. If the African Union has policies that are not just a repetition of the OAU, then it will be welcome. In a theoretical sense it is a good move, but practically, it will have to stand the test of history.

What do you think about reparations?

I believe the rich boys of the G-8 nations owe Africa a hell of a lot. Africa was looted by the so-called first world.

Take gold, for example: even today, in the year 2003, gold is taken out of South Africa and comes back to us as finished products that we buy for ten times as much. The first world owes the so-called third world. They should return our wealth in the form of injecting the continent with capital to improve the lives of the people.

Affirmative Action and Reconciliation

The affirmative action debate is heating up in South Africa. Some whites fear that they are losing opportunities to less-qualified and under-qualified blacks.

To utter hell with white fears! How can blacks be sufficiently qualified when they were never given the opportunities? Apartheid meant that black journalists were self-created because they were not university products. They came from a disadvantaged people with no resources or access to go to Grahamstown University or Rhodes University to study journalism. Most of our black journalists are self-made. So when you introduce that transformation, where do you expect to get a pool of trained journalists? Whites want gradual affirmative action, and we are nine years into liberation—but they occupy senior positions in every sphere of our lives.

Do you think the Truth and Reconciliation Commission was successful?

I don't think I should answer that. I have my own views about that.

What are they?

My view, which belongs to me, not the ANC, is that the Truth and Reconciliation Commission [TRC] will need its own Truth and Reconciliation Commission one day. I don't know how much we achieved by getting criminals to stand in the TRC, pronounce half-truths, reveal a quarter of the crimes they committed and by virtue of them presenting themselves before the TRC, they get away with murder. No one can swear that they revealed the truth of the atrocities they committed during those years. Maybe, South Africa should have gone the way of Nuremberg, where people were just tried for war crimes. What happens to the families of the victims of a man who says he doesn't even remember the number of killings he was responsible for? But because he told that truth he is given amnesty. That is the problem.

There has been an emergence of the landless people movement in South Africa. I'm curious to know what you think about it?

I was in the forefront of fighting for land. I am very sympathetic to people who are fighting for land. Our association with the land is far deeper than many people realize. When an African child is born, his or her umbilical cord is traditionally buried within the homestead, on the grounds. The relationship between persons and the land is so deep, that I cannot find faults with anyone fighting for land. That is what the Freedom Charter said in 1955: the land belongs to all who live on it and till it.

You remain very popular with the people, the grassroots, of South Africa although you're at odds with the leadership of the ANC. Do you have political ambitions of your own? Maybe someday organizing a separate party?

Do I see myself as against myself? I am the African National Congress.

But you're very critical of the ANC. . . .

I am not just critical of the African National Congress. I am also critical of myself. When I say we are not moving fast enough, I am merely speaking the truth. Not because I am part of the government. I am not going to say that the struggles of the landless people are not justified. I not going to say that HIV does not cause AIDS. I merely speak the truth. And speaking the truth does not contextualize me in any given ideology.

Has the apartheid-era passion been sucked out of the ANC

now that it is playing a leadership role in South Africa?

I wish I had an answer to that. Sometimes, I pose the same question myself. I cannot interpret what goes on in the minds of my colleagues. I would love to think that we have the same passion we had when we dug the trenches and fought in the revolution. My particular problem is that I fought in the forefront of that struggle. I fought in the revolution. I fought underground. I was so much of that struggle. It cannot be taken out of me even if I wanted to do that. That's why I still live in Soweto. I cannot divorce myself from that struggle.

Thabo Mbeki turned away from your embrace at the 25th anniversary of the Soweto Massacre in 2001. Is this conflict. . . .

It's a closed chapter now. It's history.

Legacy of a Revolutionary

What is your relationship with Nelson Mandela like now? Do you still communicate?

I never talk about that. As I've said before, I was not Mandela's product politically. Nor was he mine. Of course, it would have never worked—he's twice my age! I really don't talk about things like that. I have defined myself in terms of the revolution, my political life.

How do you want to be remembered?

I should leave that to you. Right? I don't think anyone plans that. I don't think anyone in the same position plans that. How do you even begin to define me? I don't even know how to define myself.

Do you have any regrets?

If I had to live my life again, I would start from day one and do exactly the same thing all over again. The struggle was my opium and I am still addicted to it. For as long as my people are dying of AIDS, and suffering from racism, and as long as South Africa still remains a blistering inferno of racial history, I will remain what I am.

3

Profiles · in · History

Other Nineteenth-Century Trailblazers

Maria Stewart

Marilyn Richardson

Maria Stewart (1803–1879) was a teacher, reformer, writer, and abolitionist who emerged in the Boston antislavery community amid the heated debates over black colonization. An elite group of whites had formed the American Colonization Society in 1817, which advocated the return of free blacks to Africa. Most blacks in the Northeast were vehemently opposed to colonization, viewing themselves as no longer citizens of Africa but of the United States. Stewart, a one-time house servant, lent both her mind and her voice to the anticolonization cause and other abolitionist issues. In doing so, she became the first known black woman—and possibly the first American woman of any race—to deliver a public speech in the United States. Although she essentially retired from public life in 1833, after only two years of vocally lobbying for black freedom and self-improvement, Stewart remained as committed to black rights as she was to her Christian faith. She is considered by many to be the first female political activist in the United States.

Scholar and author Marilyn Richardson, who has taught at Harvard University, the Massachusetts Institute of Technology, and Boston University, is currently principal of African-Americana Consultants with the Primary Source center for the interdisciplinary study of history and the humanities.

Marilyn Richardson, *Maria W. Stewart: America's First Black Woman Political Writer: Essays and Speeches*. Bloomington: Indiana University Press, 1987. Copyright © 1987 by Marilyn Richardson. All rights reserved. Reproduced by permission of the publisher.

In September of 1832, in Boston, Massachusetts, Maria W. Stewart, a black woman, did what no American-born woman, black or white, before her is recorded as having done. She mounted a lecture platform and raised a political argument before a "promiscuous" audience, that is, one composed of both men and women. On that particular occasion, Stewart spoke out against the colonization movement, a controversial scheme to expatriate certain black Americans to West Africa. "Why sit ye here and die?" she demanded in the characteristically challenging style familiar to those in the audience who had read her work in the abolitionist journal *The Liberator*. "If we say we will go to a foreign land, the famine and the pestilence are there, and there we shall die. If we sit here, we shall die." Hers was a call to action, urging blacks to demand their human rights from their white oppressors. At the same time, she encouraged them to plan wisely for their future in this country, to see to the establishment of strong, self-sufficient educational and economic institutions within their own community.

Stewart, the first American woman to lecture in public on political themes and leave extant copies of her texts, was a woman of profound religious faith, a pioneer black abolitionist, and a defiant champion of women's rights. Her message was unsparing and controversial, intended as a goad to her people to organize against the tyranny of slavery in the South and to resist and defy the restrictions of bigotry in the North.

Stewart's Originality

Likely the first black American to lecture in defense of women's rights, Stewart constructed a spirited series of arguments citing feminist precedents drawn from biblical, classical, and historical sources. A bold and militant orator, she called on black women to develop their highest intellectual capacities, to enter into all spheres of the life of the mind, and to participate in all activities within their community, from religion and education to politics and business, without apology to notions of female subservience. Her original synthesis of religious, abolitionist, and feminist concerns places her squarely in the forefront of a black female activist and literary tradition only now beginning to be acknowledged as of integral significance to the understanding of the history of black thought and culture in America.

During a public career in Boston of barely three years' duration, she published a political pamphlet (1831), a collection of religious meditations (1832), delivered four public lectures (1832–1833), saw her speeches printed in *The Liberator*, and finally, after moving to New York, compiled in 1834 a volume of her collected works which was published the following year. In both the formulation and the articulation of the ideas central to the emerging struggle for black freedom and human rights, Stewart was a clear forerunner to generations of the best known and most influential champions of black activism, both male and female, including Frederick Douglass, who launched his public career at the famous Nantucket meeting of 1841, Sojourner Truth, who, in 1843, began her mission of traveling and speaking for abolition and women's rights, and Frances Harper, who delivered her first public lecture, "The Elevation and Education of Our People," in New Bedford in 1854.

Life After Boston
After leaving Boston, Stewart supported herself as a teacher in New York, Baltimore, and finally, following the Civil War, in Washington, D.C. There she eventually took a position as Matron of the Freedmen's Hospital, now the Howard University Hospital. In an unexpected turn of events coming at the close of her life,

Stewart came into a modest widow's pension which she immediately invested in a new edition of her collected works. By way of preface to that 1879 volume she composed an autobiographical sketch which, through an inventive use of narrative technique, presents us with a significant and previously unexplored resource in the study of black women's literary history.

The great majority of black American women who wrote, published, and even enjoyed critical and financial success from the late eighteenth century to the middle of our own century, are best known to us through their works rather than their days. Until the biographical work now happily under way comes to further fruition, readers searching for information on black women of outstanding prominence in their eras will quickly discover the gaping spaces of lost or thinly documented years in their recorded lives. So it is with Stewart, orphaned at the age of five with no known siblings, and widowed after three years of marriage with no offspring. . . .

Early Years
Some things we know. Her young years were spent "bound out" as a servant in the household of a minister. During that period, characterized by the influence of religion and the search for knowledge and intellectual growth, Stewart gained the first-hand experience that enabled her to write so compellingly of the effects of endless toil and drudgery on the minds and spirits of those blacks in the North she would come to consider only nominally free.

Stewart's life in Boston from the 1820s to the mid-1830s, including her years as a public speaker, was influenced by the Bible, the writings of [black abolitionist] David Walker, and those of the Englishman John Adams on women's history.

Her life in New York after 1834 included membership in a black "Female Literary Society." Such organizations were vital elements in black women's cultural and intellectual history. Stewart's participation, first as beneficiary of the group's assistance and later as a contributing member, is strikingly emblematic of the role these societies played in preparing their members for positions of community leadership.

In New York, Stewart began her career as a teacher. According to a history of the Williamsburg colored school, "by 1845 more than sixty Black scholars were taught by a Maria W. Stewart." In 1847, she was appointed assistant to the school's principal, Hezekiah Green.

There is also the curious and edifying story of Stewart's later years in Washington, D.C., following the Civil War where, as a result of legislation passed in 1878, she was able to press her claim for a pension as the widow of a veteran of the War of 1812.

The body of Stewart's political writing is, however, from the first third of the nineteenth century. It is most profitably examined in the context of Boston's small but politically dynamic black community of that time, and in light of the growing abolitionist movement at the point when *The Liberator* was just coming into being.

Slavery and Degradation

Maria Stewart

Maria Stewart's speeches typically bring together her two
driving passions: black equality and Christian devoutness.
Stewart lays the blame for black oppression squarely on
the shoulders of slavery and bigots. She also challenges
the stereotype of passive black victimhood by encouraging blacks to strive for active moral and spiritual self-
improvement and steadfastness of purpose. In the following
selection, a speech Stewart delivered in 1832 at Boston's
Franklin Hall, she urges black women and men to aspire to
overcome the burden of servile toil that whites have foisted
upon them. Intertwining biblical and temporal appeals,
Stewart exhorts her fellow blacks to take initiative and har-
ness their energies toward demonstrating the human dignity denied them by slavery and prejudice. In short, she in-
vests the black community with both the responsibility and
agency to secure its own liberation.

❦   ❦   ❦

W hy sit ye here and die? If we say we will go to a
foreign land, the famine and the pestilence are there,

Maria Stewart, lecture at Franklin Hall, Boston, Massachusetts, September 21,
1832.

and there we shall die. If we sit here, we shall die. Come let us plead our cause before the whites: if they save us alive, we shall live—and if they kill us, we shall but die.

Methinks I heard a spiritual interrogation—'Who shall go forward, and take off the reproach that is cast upon the people of color? Shall it be a woman?' And my heart made this reply—'If it is thy will, be it even so, Lord Jesus!'

I have heard much respecting the horrors of slavery; but may Heaven forbid that the generality of my color throughout these United States should experience any more of its horrors than to be a servant of servants, or hewers of wood and drawers of water [Joshua 9:23]! Tell us no more of southern slavery; for with few exceptions, although I may be very erroneous in my opinion, yet I consider our condition but little better than that. Yet, after all, methinks there are no chains so galling as those that bind the soul, and exclude it from the vast field of useful and scientific knowledge. O, had I received the advantages of an early education, my ideas would, ere now, have expanded far and wide; but, alas! I possess nothing but moral capability—no teachings but the teachings of the Holy Spirit.

The Power of Prejudice

I have asked several individuals of my sex, who transact business for themselves, if providing our girls were to give them the most satisfactory references, they would not be willing to grant them an equal opportunity with others? Their reply has been—for their own part, they had no objection; but as it was not the custom, were they to take them into their employ, they would be in danger of losing the public patronage.

And such is the powerful force of prejudice. Let our girls possess whatever amiable qualities of soul they may; let their characters be fair and spotless as innocence itself; let their natural taste and ingenuity be what they may; it is impossible for scarce an individual of them to rise above the condition of servants. Ah! why is this cruel and unfeeling distinction? Is it merely because God has made our complexion to vary? If it be, O shame to soft, relenting humanity! "Tell it not in Gath! publish it not in the streets of Askelon!" [2 Samuel 1:20]. Yet, after all, methinks were the American free people of color to turn their attention more assiduously to moral worth and intellectual improvement, this would be the result: prejudice would gradually diminish, and the whites would be compelled to say, unloose those fetters!

> Though black their skins as shades of night
> Their hearts are pure, their souls are white.

Forced into Servility

Few white persons of either sex, who are calculated for anything else, are willing to spend their lives and bury their talents in performing mean, servile labor. And such is the horrible idea that I entertain respecting a life of servitude, that if I conceived of their [sic] being no possibility of my rising above the condition of servant, I would gladly hail death as a welcome messenger. O, horrible idea, indeed! to possess noble souls aspiring after high and honorable acquirements, yet confined by the chains of ignorance and poverty to lives of continual drudgery and toil. Neither do I know of any who have enriched themselves by spending their lives as house-domestics, washing windows, shaking carpets, brushing boots, or tending upon gentlemen's tables. I can but die for expressing my sentiments: and I am as willing to die by the sword as the pestilence; for I am a true born American; your blood flows in my veins, and your spirit fire my breast.

I observed a piece in the *Liberator* [a major abolitionist newspaper] a few months since, stating that the colonizationists had published a work respecting us, asserting that we were lazy and idle. I confute them on that point. Take us generally as a people, we are neither lazy nor idle; and considering how little we have to excite or stimulate us, I am almost astonished that there are so many industrious and ambitious ones to be found; although I acknowledge, with extreme sorrow, that there are some who never were and never will be serviceable to society. And have you not a similar class among yourselves?

Again. It was asserted that we were "a ragged set, crying for liberty." I reply to it, the whites have so long and so loudly proclaimed the theme of equal rights and privileges, that our souls have caught the flame also, ragged as we are. As far as our merit deserves, we feel a common desire to rise above the condition of servants and drudges. I have learnt, by bitter experience, that continual hard labor deadens the energies of the soul, and benumbs the faculties of the mind; the ideas become confined, the mind barren, and, like the scorching sands of Arabia, produces nothing; or like the uncultivated soil, brings forth thorns and thistles.

Denied Opportunities

Again, continual and hard labor irritates our tempers and sours our dispositions; the whole system becomes worn out with toil and fatigue; nature herself becomes almost exhausted, and we care but little whether we live or die. It is true, that the free people of color throughout these United States are neither bought nor sold, nor under the lash of the cruel driver; many obtain a comfortable support; but few, if any, have an opportunity of becoming rich and independent; and the enjoyments we most pursue are as unprofitable to us as the spider's web or the floating bubbles that vanish into air.

As servants, we are respected; but let us presume to aspire any higher, our employer regards us no longer. And were it not that the King eternal has declared that Ethiopia shall stretch forth her hands unto God, I should indeed despair.

I do not consider it derogatory, my friends, for persons to live out to service. There are many whose inclination leads them to aspire no higher; and I would highly commend the performance of almost anything for an honest livelihood; but where constitutional strength is wanting, labor of this kind, in its mildest form, is painful. And doubtless many are the prayers that have ascended to Heaven from Afric's daughters for strength to perform their work. Oh, many are the tears that have been shed for the want of that strength! Most of our color have dragged out a miserable existence of servitude from the cradle to the grave. And what literary acquirement can be made, or useful knowledge derived, from either maps, books, or charts, by those who continually drudge from Monday morning until Sunday noon? O, ye fairer sisters, whose hands are never soiled, whose nerves and muscles are never strained, go learn by experience! Had we had the opportunity that you have had, to improve our moral and mental faculties, what would have hindered our intellects from being as bright, and our manners from being as dignified as yours? Had it been our lot to have been nursed in the lap of affluence and ease, and to have basked beneath the smiles and sunshine of fortune, should we not have naturally supposed that we were never made to toil? And why are not our forms as delicate, and our constitutions as slender, as yours? Is not the workmanship as curious and complete? Have pity upon us, have pity upon us, O ye who have hearts to feel for other's woes; for the hand of God has touched us. Owing to the disadvantages under which we labor, there are many flowers among us that are

> . . . born to bloom unseen
> And waste their fragrance on the desert air.

A Call for Initiative

My beloved brethren, as Christ has died in vain for those who will not accept his offered mercy, so will it be vain for the advocates of freedom to spend their breath in our behalf, unless with united hearts and souls you make some mighty efforts to raise your sons and daughters from the horrible state of servitude and degradation in which they are placed. It is upon you that woman depends; she can do but little besides using her influence; and it is for her sake and yours that I have come forward and made myself a hissing and a reproach among the people [Jeremiah 29:18]; for I am also one of the wretched and miserable daughters of the descendants of fallen Africa. Do you ask, why are you wretched and miserable? I reply, look at many of the most worthy and most interesting of us doomed to spend our lives in gentlemen's kitchens. Look at our young men, smart, active and energetic, with souls filled with ambitious fire; if they look forward, alas! What are their prospects? They can be nothing but the humblest laborers, on account of their dark complexions; hence many of them lose their ambition, and become worthless. Look at our middle-aged men, clad in their rusty plaids and coats; in winter, every cent they earn goes to buy their wood and pay their rents; the poor wives also toil beyond their strength, to help support their families. Look at our aged sires, whose heads are whitened with the frosts of seventy winters, with their old wood-saws on their backs. Alas, what keeps us so? Prejudice, ignorance and poverty. But ah! methinks our oppression is soon to come to an end; yea, before the Majesty of heaven, our groans and cries have reached the ears of the Lord of

Sabaoth [James 5:4]. As the prayers and tears of Christians will avail the finally impenitent nothing; neither will the prayers and tears of the friends of humanity avail us anything, unless we possess a spirit of virtuous emulation within our breasts. Did the pilgrims, when they first landed on these shores, quietly compose themselves and say, "The Britons have all the money and all the power, and we must continue their servants forever?" Did they sluggishly sigh and say, "Our lot is hard, the Indians own the soil, and we cannot cultivate it?" No; they first made powerful efforts to raise themselves, and then God raised up those illustrious patriots, WASHINGTON and LAFAYETTE, to assist and defend them. And, my brethren, have you made a powerful effort? Have you prayed the legislature for mercy's sake to grant you all the rights and privileges of free citizens, that your daughters may rise to that degree of respectability which true merit deserves, and your sons above the servile situations which most of them fill?

Sojourner Truth

Elizabeth Shafer

Preacher, antislavery activist, and feminist Sojourner Truth was born a slave named Isabella Baumfree in 1797 in Ulster County, New York. As an adult and free woman, she adopted her new name as homage to her life's mission: as a traveler, even a pilgrim, for truth, as Elizabeth Shafer explains in the following biographical selection. For all her sincere religious piety, Sojourner Truth saw "truth" in primarily earthly and practical terms, realizable through slavery's abolition, women's right to vote, and love for one's fellow humans. Shafer also discusses Truth's determined pursuit of tangible, common-sense solutions to personal challenges, whether successfully suing for her son's emancipation or publicly baring her breasts to silence a white male heckler who was rudely questioning her gender.

Elizabeth Shafer is the author of "Sojourner Truth: 'A Self-Made Woman,'" as well as the writer of a sourcebook for teaching J.K. Rowlings's *Harry Potter* books.

❦　❦　❦

She was over 6 feet tall, rawboned, black, and—for the first forty years of her life—a slave. The next forty-six years she spent becoming, as she said, "a self-made woman."

Sojourner Truth was a powerful and eloquent speaker against slavery and for women's rights, lecturing in twenty-one states and the District of Columbia from 1843 until 1878, when she was 81. She was a friend and coworker of the great names among the abolitionists and fighters for women's rights. She was a guest of Harriet Beecher Stowe, who celebrated her as "The Libyan Sibyl" in *The Atlantic Monthly*; and she was received at the White House by Abraham Lincoln.

Those who heard her speak and sing in her deep, strong voice never forgot her nor her shrewd wit, simple wisdom, and droll humor. Mrs. Stowe wrote of the "power and sweetness in that great warm soul and that vigorous frame," adding, "I do not recall ever to have been conversant with anyone who had more of that silent and subtle power which we call personal presence than this woman." From the sister of the famous preacher and spellbinder, Henry Ward Beecher, this was the ultimate compliment.

Slave Named Isabella

She was born in 1797 in Ulster County, New York, the twelfth child of Bomefree and Mama Bett, slaves of a Dutchman, Charles Hardenbergh. (New York and New Jersey were the last of the northern states to keep slaves; the other states had abolished slavery following the Revolution.) When Sojourner was about 11, Hardenbergh died, and "Isabella," as she was then called, was sold at an auction of "slaves, horses, and other cattle" to a Yankee storekeeper, John Nealy. Nealy paid a hundred dollars for the gawky child and a herd of sheep.

Years later she was to say, "Now the war begun." For Isabella spoke only Low Dutch, and the Nealys spoke only English. When her father learned how they beat her, he begged a local tavernkeeper to buy her. She lived eighteen months with the Scrivers, working in the house and in the fields and serving customers in the tavern. She was 13 now, and already 6 feet tall.

She was happy those brief months, but in 1810 John J. Dumont of nearby New Paltz bought her for $300. (As a sturdy young woman, her value was going up.) Dumont was a large slaveholder by New York standards, keeping ten slaves. They all lived in a large room behind the kitchen called the slave kitchen.

Isabella was a good worker—too good in the opinion of her fellow slaves, who called her "white man's nigger." She fell in love with "Catlin's Robert," as slaves were identified in those days. But Robert's master beat him terribly and forced him to marry one of the Catlin slaves. Isabella, in turn, was married to old Thomas, one of Dumont's slaves. They were to have five children.

While she was chiefly a house slave for Mrs. Dumont, she also worked in the fields. She would put her latest baby in a basket, tie a rope to the handles, and suspend it in a tree, where a small child was set to swinging it.

A Hope of Freedom

Meanwhile, New York State had passed a new law. All slaves born before July 4, 1799, were to be freed on July 4, 1827. All slaves younger than 28 were "free"—but had to work as unpaid servants until the boys were 28, the girls 25. Because she was such a faithful worker, Dumont promised Isabella he would free her a year early. But in the summer of 1826, he refused to fulfill his promise.

Isabella remembered the Quaker, Levi Rowe, who had said to her once, years before, "Thou should not be a slave." She took her youngest child, Sophia, leaving the others at Dumont's with Thomas, and walked to Rowe's farm.

Rowe was dying, but he sent her on to Mr. and Mrs.

Isaac S. Van Wagener. When Dumont followed, demanding his property, the Van Wageners agreed to buy Isabella's services for the rest of the year for twenty dollars, and the child's services until she was 25 for five dollars. However, they instructed Isabella not to call them "master" and "mistress," and she was treated as a paid servant.

Personal Relationship with God

Once she became homesick and almost agreed to accompany Dumont back to his farm, but as she was heading for the gate she heard a voice: "Not another step!" She quickly returned to her room, where she prayed for strength. Her mother had long ago taught her the Lord's prayer in Low Dutch, and had told her solemnly, "There is a God, who hears and sees you." It was at this crisis in her life that Isabella discovered Jesus. But she was afraid, she said afterwards, that the whites would discover that Jesus was her friend and take him from her as they had taken everything else, so she kept her new friend a secret.

There was a small island in a nearby stream. Here she wove a wall of willows and conducted private talks with God and Jesus. She was to continue this very personal dialog for the rest of her life.

On "freedom day," July 4, 1827, Isaac and Maria Van Wagener conducted a small private ceremony, reading from the Bible. Maria kissed Isabella on the cheek. "Take thy Sophia, too, into freedom," she said, handing her the child. They agreed upon wages for her labor, and Isabella and the child lived with them for another two years.

Suing for a Son's Liberty

Her son, Peter, had disappeared, and Isabella finally learned that Dumont had sold the boy to a family whose daughter had taken Peter south to Alabama. This meant, of course, that he would never be free.

When Isabella spoke to Mrs. Dumont about Peter, the woman jeered at her. Isabella drew herself to her full height and cried in her deep voice, "I'll have my child again!" She was to recall afterwards, "When I spoke to my mistress that way. I felt so tall within. I felt as if the power of a nation was within me."

An abolitionist advised her to go to a certain Quaker for help. She arrived at night, and was given a room of her own with a tall poster bed. She remembered later, "I was scared when she left me alone with that great white bed. I had never been in a real bed in my life. It never came into my mind she could mean me to sleep on it. So I just camped under it, and I slept pretty well there on the floor."

Next morning, she took her case to the grand jury at Kingston. This was the first of many battles she was to undertake and win. The woman who was to become Sojourner Truth believed in the power of the law and used it effectively for herself and her people.

Peter was returned to her, and the two went to New York City in 1829. But the boy fell into bad company and she was forced to send him to sea. He sent her several letters, saying he had received none of her. Then he stopped writing: she never heard from him again.

The Birth of "Sojourner"

While in New York she learned English, which she always spoke with a heavy Dutch accent, and worked as a domestic for various families and for a religious group called The Kingdom. But in 1843, she had a vision. She took her clothes, some bread and cheese, and twenty-five cents for the ferry to Brooklyn. "I am no longer Isabella," she said. "I am Sojourner." But Sojourner what? She gave the matter some thought. Remembering that a slave always took the name of her master, she said, "Oh, God, thou art my last master, and thy name is Truth, so shall Truth be my abiding name until I die."

And so, at 46, Sojourner Truth was born.

The year 1843 was a time of great religious revival. Reform was in the air. Abolitionists were calling for an end to slavery. Talk of women's rights would culminate in the first Women's Rights Convention at Seneca, New York, in 1848. Men and women were setting up religious communities. Camp meetings were held everywhere.

In her wanderings, Sojourner came upon her first camp meeting. She began to speak and sing at many

"Ain't I a Woman?"

Sojourner Truth was a prominent advocate for both abolition and women's voting rights. At the 1851 Women's Rights Convention in Akron, Ohio, she delivered an extemporaneous speech that came to be known as "Ain't I a Woman?" and a rallying cry for nineteenth-century feminists.

Well, children, where there is so much racket there must be something out of kilter. I think that 'twixt the negroes of the South and the women at the North, all talking about rights, the white men will be in a fix pretty soon. But what's all this here talking about?

That man over there says that women need to be helped into carriages, and lifted over ditches, and to have the best place everywhere. Nobody ever helps me into carriages, or over mud-puddles, or gives me any best place! And ain't I a woman? Look at me! Look at my arm! I have ploughed and planted, and gathered into barns, and no man could head me! And ain't I a woman? I could work as much and eat as much as a man—when I could get it—and bear the lash as well! And ain't I a woman? I have borne thirteen children, and seen most all sold off to such gatherings. Later, she advertised and conducted meetings of her own. Olive Gilbert, who was the first to help Sojourner put her story into print (*Narrative of Sojourner Truth: A Northern Slave*, 1850) commented, "All who have ever heard her sing . . . will probably remember it as long as they remember her."

At one such camp meeting, a group of rowdies threatened to disrupt the proceedings. Sojourner walked to one side, on a little knoll, and began to sing. The rowdies gathered around her, begging her to sing some more, and became quiet. They even laughed appreciatively when she told them, "Well, there are two con-

slavery, and when I cried out with my mother's grief, none but Jesus heard me! And ain't I a woman?

Then they talk about this thing in the head; what's this they call it? [Member of audience whispers, "intellect."] That's it, honey. What's that got to do with women's rights or negroes' rights? If my cup won't hold but a pint, and yours holds a quart, wouldn't you be mean not to let me have my little half measure full?

Then that little man in black there, he says women can't have as much rights as men, 'cause Christ wasn't a woman! Where did your Christ come from? Where did your Christ come from? From God and a woman! Man had nothing to do with Him.

If the first woman God ever made was strong enough to turn the world upside down all alone, these women together ought to be able to turn it back, and get it right side up again! And now they is asking to do it, the men better let them.

Obliged to you for hearing me, and now old Sojourner ain't got nothing more to say.

Sojourner Truth, "Ain't I a Woman?" Speech delivered at the Women's Rights Convention, Akron, Ohio, December 1851.

gregations on this ground. It is written that the sheep shall be separated from the goats. The other preachers have the sheep, I have the goats. I have a few sheep among my goats, but they are very ragged." Both meetings went on without incident after that.

Truth and Other Reformers

She met all the great figures of the abolition movement: Samuel Hill, Wendell Phillips. Parker Pillsbury, Frederick Douglass, and William Lloyd Garrison. These men also worked with women in organizing the first women's rights convention.

Sojourner knew Lucretia Mott, Susan B. Anthony, Elizabeth Cady Stanton, and Lucy Stone. She was the only black delegate to the Worcester, Massachusetts, women's rights convention in 1850. Men jeered, newspapers called it the Hen Convention, and one minister even threatened to expel from his congregation any member daring to attend.

It was at this convention that Sojourner, ever the militant, asked, "If women want any rights more'n they've got, why don't they just take 'em and not be talking about it?"

She was a faithful fighter for all women's rights, but she drew the line at the current fad of wearing "bloomers." Recalling her days as a slave who got only a single length of cloth to cover her long frame and so had to stitch up the legs for modesty, she declared, "Tell *you*, I had enough of bloomers in them days!"

Lecturing for Abolition

With the passage of the Fugitive Slave Act in 1850, the abolitionists redoubled their activities. Sojourner was invited to join them on their speaking tours.

She often traveled alone, in a borrowed buggy loaded with copies of her book, song sheets of her own composing, and copies of her photograph ("I sell the shadow to support the substance.") She would give the horse its head, saying, "God, you drive." It always seemed to turn out right. She would stop at a cross-roads or in a village square, unfold the freedom banner which the Akron, Ohio, women's rights convention had given her, and speak and sing.

One of her own songs, eleven stanzas long, began:

> I am pleading for my people—
> A poor, down-trodden race,
> Who dwell in freedom's boasted land
> With no abiding place.
>
> I am pleading that my people
> May have their rights restored,
> For they have long been toiling
> And yet have no reward.

Uncle Tom's Cabin had received instant acclaim in 1852, and, wanting to meet the author, Sojourner appeared at Harriet Beecher Stowe's home in Andover, Massachusetts. Harriet was so taken with her visitor that she invited her to stay for several days.

"An audience was what she wanted." Harriet was to write later. "It mattered not whether high or low, learned or ignorant. She had things to say, and was ready to say them at all times, and to anyone."

"Ain't I a Woman?"

In 1857 the *Dred Scott* decision ruled that a slave could not be a citizen, and that Congress had no power to exclude slavery from the western territories. This precipitated new abolitionist activity. Sojourner went into Indiana with Parker Pillsbury. It was during this speaking tour that a hostile doctor rose and demanded that she show her breasts to a group of women from the audience. He said, "Your voice is not the voice of a woman, it is the voice of a man, and we believe you are a man."

Silently, Sojourner Truth, now 60, undid her Quaker kerchief and opened her dress, displaying her breasts to the whole congregation. "It is not my shame but yours that I do this," she said.

Events began moving more swiftly now. In 1859, John Brown raided Harpers Ferry. In 1860, Lincoln was elected President. And by April 1861, Fort Sumter had been fired upon.

Civil War Activism

Josephine Griffing of Ohio asked Sojourner to accompany her on an anti-slavery lecture tour into Indiana, where Copperheads (pro-slavery forces) controlled the legislature. This was a dangerous undertaking, but Sojourner agreed at once. Two miles across the Ohio-Indiana border, she was arrested. Josephine got a court order for her release. Hecklers broke up their first meeting and they were taken into protective custody by a member of the Union home guard, who escorted them to Angola. Here, the Copperheads threatened to burn the building where Sojourner was to speak.

"Then I will speak upon the ashes," she said firmly.

The women of the town dressed her in a red, white, and blue shawl with a sash and apron to match. She wore a cap with a star, and a star on each shoulder.

Sojourner remembered:

> When we were ready to go, they put me into a large, beautiful carriage with the captain and other gentlemen, all of whom were armed. The soldiers walked by our side and a long procession followed. As we neared the court house, looking out of the window I saw that the building was surrounded by a great crowd. I felt as I was going against the Philistines and I prayed the Lord to deliver me out of their hands. But when the rebels saw such a mighty army coming, they fled, and by the time we arrived they were scattered over the fields, looking like a flock of fright-

ened crows, and not one was left but a small boy, who sat upon the fence, crying, "Nigger, nigger!"

The procession marched into the court house, everyone sang, and she spoke without interruption.

The tour was a triumph, but it exhausted her. She was ill for some time, and there were rumors she was dead. But the Emancipation Proclamation of January 1, 1863, heartened her; she declared that she must get well.

A Friend of the Union

Slowly, over the years, she had been gathering her family about her in Battle Creek, Michigan—her daughters and grandsons Sammy and James, who sometimes acted as escorts on her journeys. When she was not lecturing, she earned her living as she always did, cooking, cleaning house, doing laundry, and caring for the sick.

Grandson James Caldwell had joined the Union Army now that they were accepting Negroes. At Thanksgiving in 1863, Sojourner visited the 1st Michigan Colored Infantry at Detroit, taking them donations of good things to eat. She taught them to sing her latest song, to the tune of *John Brown's Body:*

We are the valiant soldiers who've 'listed for the war;
We are fighting for the Union, we are fighting for
the law;
We can shoot a rebel farther than a white man ever
saw.
As we go marching on. . . .

From Detroit, she went to New York, speaking to Henry Ward Beecher's Brooklyn congregation at Plymouth Church. And on October 29, 1864, she met Abraham Lincoln at the White House. The President signed her "Book of Life," an autograph book containing the signatures of many of the most famous people of her time.

She found plenty to do in Washington. She spoke to

the Colored Soldiers' Aid Society. She worked at Arlington Heights, Virginia as a counselor for the National Freedmen's Relief Association, and that autumn she was asked to help the surgeon in charge of the Freedmen's Hospital to "promote order, cleanliness, industry, and virtue among the patients."

Fighting Segregation

Before the war, the streetcars in Washington had been segregated. After Lincoln signed a law outlawing discrimination in Washington public transportation, many conductors simply refused to stop for black passengers. One day Sojourner Truth stood in the middle of the street and shouted three times at the top of her lungs, "I WANT TO RIDE!" She nearly panicked the horses, but she managed to get on, then refused to stand on the platform behind the horses, "I am a passenger and shall sit with the other passengers."

In a later incident, an irate conductor slammed her against the door, pushing her shoulder out of joint. Again, she went to court. The Freedmen's Bureau lawyer sued the company, the conductor lost his job, and from then on blacks rode the Washington streetcars.

In 1867, escorted by grandson Sammy, she traveled through western New York, seeking jobs for freed slaves. Journalist Theodore Tilton asked permission to write her life story. She replied, "I am not ready to be writ up yet, for I have still lots to accomplish." And in 1870 she set out on "the last great mission of her life"— petitioning Congress for free land for the former slaves. But Senator Charles Sumner, who had worked for passage of the bill, died. Then grandson Sammy fell ill and died. Sojourner herself suffered a stroke and a lengthy illness. The petition for free land failed, one of the few failures in her long and productive life.

In the nation's centennial year, she celebrated her

eightieth birthday. Her paralysis had disappeared, her hair began to grow in black instead of its former gray, and as writers of the period commented, her deep voice had lost none of its power. When she was 81, she spoke in thirty-six different towns in her home state of Michigan. And in July of that year, she was one of three Michigan delegates to the 30th anniversary meeting of the Women's Rights Convention.

While her dream of free land had not been realized, she was to see 60,000 freedmen take up homesteads in Kansas by the end of 1879.

Sojourner Truth died at her home in Battle Creek on November 26, 1883, with her family around her. She was buried at Oak Hill Cemetery. Many of her early friends were dead or too old to attend the services, but Frederick Douglass sent a message, as did Wendell Phillips. A thousand friends and neighbors filed past her coffin. Among the floral offerings was a great sheaf of ripened wheat from the freedmen of Kansas.

Once when a friend had asked, "But Sojourner, what if there is no heaven?" she had replied, "What will I say if I don't get there? Why, I'll say, 'Bless the Lord! I had a good time thinking I would!'"

Mary Ann Shadd Cary

Jane Rhodes

The Fugitive Slave Law of 1850 extended a similar 1793
law that established the right of owners, their agents, and
federal authorities to seize runaway slaves in free states and
to obligate private citizens to help recapture refugees from
slavery. The 1850 law was applauded by southern slave interests but was fiercely decried throughout the North. Free
blacks as well as fugitives were jeopardized by the law's refusal of most legal means by which an individual might
prove his or her freedom, such as the right to call witnesses
and be tried by a jury. Many black abolitionists, such as
groundbreaking lawyer, journalist, and educator Mary Ann
Shadd Cary, urged blacks to immigrate to Canada, already
a haven for thousands of former slaves who had escaped
north via the Underground Railroad. The following selection by Jane Rhodes profiles Shadd Cary, the first black
woman to attend law school at Howard University as well
as the first female newspaper editor on the continent.

   Jane Rhodes teaches in the department of ethnic studies
at the University of California, San Diego, specializing in
race, gender, and media.

Jane Rhodes, *Mary Ann Shadd Cary: The Black Press and Protest in the Nineteenth
Century*. Bloomington: Indiana University Press, 1998. Copyright © 1998 by Jane
Rhodes. All rights reserved. Reproduced by permission.

On Independence Day 1856, Frederick Douglass took time out from his agonizing over the violence in "Bleeding Kansas" to praise Mary Ann Shadd Cary as an exemplar. "We do not know her equal among the colored ladies of the United States," Douglass proclaimed in the pages of his newspaper. Shadd Cary, founder and publisher of the *Provincial Freeman*, had toiled away in relative obscurity in the black expatriate communities of Canada. Douglass wanted his readers to know something of her "unceasing industry, . . . unconquerable zeal and commendable ability." Paradoxically, Douglass also saw fit to note in his tribute that "The tone of her paper has been at times harsh and complaining."

This seeming contradiction—that Shadd Cary would be viewed simultaneously as an object of respect and leadership, and as an object of derision—is central to the story of this African American woman. Mary Ann Shadd Cary was clearly an exceptional figure in United States history: first black woman to publish and edit a newspaper, second to become an attorney, champion of black emigration to Canada, educator, orator, feminist, and agitator for civil rights. She devoted her life to using public discourse to advance a range of political and social reforms. In the process she became a consummate communicator who thrust herself into a public sphere where few people of color, especially women, dared to tread.

Such accomplishments could only be attained by someone with a strong character, keen intelligence, and determination. But Shadd Cary was neither a saint nor a heroine in any romantic sense. This was a woman with her share of human faults; she could be headstrong, cantankerous, and abrasive in her personal and public relations. She was motivated by both altruism and self-

aggrandizement, by political philosophy and a quick
temper. She enjoyed the sports of debate and repartee,
and rarely hesitated to strike back at rivals and enemies.
These qualities, while often admired in a man, were
scorned in a woman, making her both the subject and
source of controversy. Mary Ann Shadd Cary was a
quintessential dissident; a woman whose life was marked
by the numerous ways she transgressed the boundaries
of sex, color, and class, and the price she paid for the
boldness of her actions.

The Rise of the Black Press

An evaluation of Shadd Cary's career as a publisher and
editor transforms the traditional conceptual framework
of nineteenth-century journalism as a white male-
centered enterprise where women and persons of color
existed only at the margins. James Carey has suggested
that the black press is more than "a source of data about
Black social history," but rather a means for understanding the cultural milieu of the African American experience. The black press emerged at a particular historical
moment during which the partisan press was moving toward commercialization, while the nation's political and
social practices were devoted to denying freedom of expression to people of color. The nineteenth-century
black press played a crucial role in community building,
and was an influential forum for the assertion and dis-
semination of African Americans' ideas. Shadd Cary's
paper, the *Provincial Freeman*, was one of the longest-
operating independent black newspapers of the antebellum period, and was instrumental in the community debates over abolition and emigration. Shadd Cary's
efforts to keep the newspaper going reveal the tenuous
nature of nineteenth-century African American economic institutions, and the barriers to the articulation of
African American political ideas. The *Provincial Freeman*

has been an important resource in the study of African American history, but Shadd Cary's significance as the driving force behind the paper has been obscured.

A Nationalist and Feminist

The life of this public figure can also be defined, in large part, by her participation in African American political movements before and after the Civil War. Yet, it is difficult to place Mary Ann Shadd Cary as an historical subject; she does not fit our contemporary expectations of what a radical abolitionist, feminist, or black nationalist should be. Shadd Cary consistently defied the conventions and strategies of the movements in which she was involved. From her upbringing in an activist family, and vantage point as a teacher in embattled all-black schools, she developed a powerful commitment to the cause of black liberation and empowerment. But she was equally critical of the social and political practices she observed in black communities. Shadd Cary was an early nationalist who shied away from masculinist, Afrocentric ideologies; she forged a distinct perspective on black American autonomy and survival that put her at odds with many of her contemporaries. Her evolving intellectual positions paralleled the changing circumstances of African American life—from the hopelessness of the 1850s, to optimism following the war, and the dismantling of the gains of Reconstruction. Shadd Cary was an activist who could deeply love black people, while simultaneously fighting with them over the personal and the political.

Mary Ann Shadd Cary appears prominently in what continues to be the definitive study of early black nationalist and emigrationist movements, and her writing has been reproduced in several documentary sourcebooks. Recent scholarship has claimed a place for her within the small but vibrant community of nineteenth-century black women activists. But the quest to establish nineteenth-century black women's political identity has resulted in the construction of Shadd Cary as part of a collectivity—an imagined community of activists who shared common experiences of oppression and privilege as part of the black intelligentsia. It is equally important to see Shadd Cary as an activist who was not necessarily part of an established network of antebellum black women. It was not until after the Civil War that she began to participate in women's associational politics through the temperance and suffrage movements. At the end of her life she had developed an appreciation for the potential of black women's collective action, but did not live to see the club movement come to fruition.

Early in her activist life, Shadd Cary became determined to have some control over the public representations of her concepts, ideas, and feelings. She understood the intersection between public discourse and political and social action, and waged a constant battle to be heard. She sought to present herself as an authoritative, learned source who had a valuable opinion about the future of her people. When strategically necessary, she also represented herself as an embattled victim, or as an innocent woman enduring attacks on her virtue. She deliberately manipulated gendered notions of propriety to gain a sympathetic audience or to inspire outrage against her foes. Some considered her a visionary, others saw her as arrogant and presumptuous. But Shadd Cary believed she was fashioning a representative identity that would enable her to have a public voice. Her peers Frederick Douglass and Martin Delany each struggled to obtain the critical authority to call themselves race leaders. Douglass was the most successful in defining himself as the nineteenth-century's representative black man. In this role, Douglass took it upon himself to anoint Shadd Cary as a representative black woman, thus complementing her own efforts at image-making. But Douglass's ambivalent Fourth of July commentary was typical of the representations of Shadd Cary constructed throughout her life. Even her most ardent supporters often expressed discomfort with her political positions and the way she expressed them. Her independence and radical positions did not fit the representative role she was expected to fulfill.

Gender and the Black Activist Community

The shifting gender dynamics within nineteenth-century African American communities provide another theme found throughout Shadd Cary's narrative. Several scholars have succinctly described the contradictions between black men's desire to keep women within the cult of domesticity and their encouragement of black women's political labor. The male impulse to privatize women created contradictory . . . spaces through which female public figures like Shadd Cary had to negotiate. This cannot be reduced to a simple male/female opposition, however. Shadd Cary's closest political allies and defenders were influential men, including Douglass, Delany, William Still, and Samuel Ringgold Ward. At times she seemed to thrive on her singular status in the company of men, and she was often critical of what she considered to be black women's capitulation to the gender conventions that constrained them. We can trace her developing politics from the antebellum era, when she muted her feminist voice in favor of abolition and emigration, to Reconstruction and its aftermath, when women's rights was in the foreground of her political agenda. Throughout this ideological progression, Shadd Cary articulated for herself and for other nineteenth-century women a sense of anger at and frustration with the gender conventions of her times. Ironically, perhaps, she has not always been recognized as a paradigmatic African American feminist.

Shadd Cary left her imprint on many of the decisive

issues that shaped the nineteenth century: slavery and abolition, black nationalism, public education, freedom of expression, woman suffrage, and temperance. Yet, her name does not resonate with popular recognition. The folklore surrounding famous nineteenth-century black women like Harriet Tubman and Sojourner Truth originated during their lives. They were heroic, distinctive figures who captured the public imagination. These women were easy to exoticize by a white public preoccupied with their illiteracy and slave status. At the same time, they were venerated by a black public enamored of their deeds and courage. Through the generations, their names have become synonymous with crucial moments in American history.

A Neglected Heroine

Mary Ann Shadd Cary, on the other hand, does not easily fit the mythologies that would have facilitated her place in historical memory. She and her contemporaries, Frances Ellen Watkins Harper, Charlotte Forten, and Sarah Parker Remond, were freeborn, educated, and thoroughly European in their outlook and in their bearing. As [historian] Nell Painter notes, these women forced whites to "reevaluate their stereotypes about black women" because they lacked the "otherness" that made a figure like Truth such a resilient folk hero. Shadd Cary was a trailblazer and a pioneer in many pursuits, but these activities tended to be outside the realm of folklore construction—hers is less a tale of bravery or cunning, and more a narrative of tenacity, political acumen, and striving for social change under difficult circumstances. There is little room in the pantheon of heroes for a black woman who simultaneously fought for—and with—her people.

Shadd Cary is a lesser known figure for other reasons, as well. A large contingent of the Shadd clan emigrated to Canada in Mary Ann's footsteps, and remained there after she returned to the United States. Many of her descendants—particularly those interested in celebrating their family tree—have done so from an Afro-Canadian perspective. Nevertheless, Shadd Cary was more fortunate than most nineteenth-century black Americans, whose stories have been lost. As a journalist, lawyer, and activist she left behind a collection of writing that provides a window on her life, her political ideas, and the world around her. Few nineteenth-century African American women produced a written record that has survived the passage of time. This lack of documentary sources has been a key obstacle in the writing of black women's history. Only a handful of well-known figures, like Ida Wells-Barnett and Elizabeth Keckley, managed to produce diaries or autobiographies that have survived to the present. In Shadd Cary's case, the gaps in the historical record make it difficult to develop a full profile of her life, but what exists is a rich resource for expanding our knowledge of the nineteenth-century black experience.

Nineteenth-Century Black Social Identity

Shadd Cary's story offers glimpses into the everyday lives of the northern black elite. The Shadd family like most of their counterparts, existed in a quasi-free status in which they enjoyed considerable privileges compared with the majority of black Americans. But, as [historian] Ira Berlin has noted, they were a despised class who "straddled one of hell's elusive boundaries." Shadd Cary's existence was shaped by discrimination and injustice, a constant struggle against poverty, and intergroup discord. At the same time she enjoyed the rare opportunities to obtain an education, practice several professions, travel extensively, engage in politics, and make independent choices about how to live her life. Both intentionally and unwittingly, her public work exemplified the crises within this aggrieved community, including the divisions between freeborn and former slave, radical nationalist and integrationist, light-skinned and dark, male and female. Her speeches and articles criticized what she saw as the "complexional character" of black American social and political structures, and she fought tirelessly for racial unity and self-sufficiency. Yet, her own actions were at times divisive. Shadd Cary was also among a minority of black activists who openly criticized the racism and paternalism manifest by many white abolitionists and reformers. Despite a growing body of literature, we still know far too little about the northern black experience both before and after the Civil War. Much of this scholarship places male figures like Douglass and Martin Delany at the center. . . .

This does not mean that Shadd Cary has been entirely ignored. In the last twenty years several essays and articles on her life have been published in textbooks, encyclopedias, and anthologies. Students of African American and women's history have long acknowledged her importance. We can trace interest in Shadd Cary to several references in women's history texts that sought to identify significant black pioneers. Her image graces the pages of black history month calendars, posters celebrating "great black foremothers," and even a card game of "great women." Recently, her spirit is evoked as a minor character in a novel about another of her contemporaries, Mary Ellen Pleasant. . . .

Shadd Cary's Living Legacy

[Since the mid-1980s], Mary Ann Shadd Cary has been assigned folk hero status in Ontario. Her work as founder and editor of the *Provincial Freemen*, and as a feminist, educator, and reformer, has been celebrated through the efforts of local historians and her descendants. In 1987, for example, the city of Toronto dedicated a new public school in her name. Writings about her work are prominently displayed in women's bookstores, and avidly discussed in history classes. Shadd Cary's articles and essays have been reproduced in assorted anthologies, and there is even a song in her honor written by Toronto-born folksinger Faith Nolan.

It remains to be seen whether Mary Ann Shadd Cary will receive as much attention in the United States. The story of her life and the world in which she lived reminds us of the halting progress this nation has made to rectify the prejudice and discrimination rooted in its history. At the same time, it reveals how far there is to go. Many of the questions about rights and freedom that she raised more than a century ago are still contested issues. In an 1856 editorial in the *Provincial Freeman*, she challenged the opponents of black emigration to take stock of the nation they refused to abandon. Her words, deemed radical in her day, ring eerily true for the present:

> Cease to uphold the United States government, if it will, and while it does uphold human slavery. Cease to grapple after the shadow while you disregard the substance. "Come out from" a government that begins its depredations upon the rights of colored men, and ends by destroying the liberties of white men: if they will not regard the members of the household, think you they will listen to you?

Several generations in the future, black feminist author Audre Lorde echoed Shadd Cary's sentiments when she proclaimed "the master's tools will never dismantle the master's house."

Profiles · in · History

Black Women and the Fight Against Racial Segregation

Mary Church Terrell

Lynne Olson

At the dawn of the twentieth century, black codes designed to segregate African Americans and deny them the rights ostensibly guaranteed by the Thirteenth, Fourteenth, and Fifteenth Amendments were firmly entrenched across the South. Racial discrimination and prejudice were rampant throughout the nation. As many leading black abolitionists such as Frederick Douglass and John Mercer Langston had foreseen, emancipation was only the first, necessary step in the long struggle for equality.

Among black activists, differences existed as to the direction the collective quest for civil rights ought to take. Eminent educator Booker T. Washington advocated "industrial education," schooling that emphasized acquisition of practical skills such as agriculture and trade to better enable blacks to compete economically with whites. Vehemently opposed to Washington's ideas, which he viewed as overly accommodating the racist status quo, was W.E.B. Du Bois, a Harvard-educated intellectual. Du Bois espoused direct initiative and agitation by black citizens in demanding full social and political equality. Out of Du Bois's Niagara Movement (cofounded with William M. Trotter in 1905) emerged the National Association for the Advancement of Colored People (NAACP) in 1909, which would endure as

Lynne Olson, *Freedom's Daughters: The Unsung Heroines of the Civil Rights Movement from 1830 to 1970*. New York: Scribner, 2001. Copyright © 2001 by Lynne Olson. All rights reserved. Reproduced by permission.

the leading civil rights organization for black Americans of the century. Among the founding members of both the Niagara Movement and the NAACP was educator, feminist, and activist Mary Church Terrell (1863–1954). The following selection by author and journalist Lynne Olson profiles Terrell and her lifetime of achievements as a leader in the battle for civil rights for blacks and women.

❧   ❧   ❧

Like an accelerating train, the fight to end institutionalized racism in America picked up more and more speed after World War II. It would gain a monumental victory in 1954, when the Supreme Court ruled on a school-desegregation case entitled *Brown v. Board of Education.* The court's decision in *Brown* provided the fuse for the modern civil rights movement. In little more than a decade, American society would be transformed.

It was perhaps predictable that the first major battle of the postwar civil rights struggle would be waged over the public schools of the South, where "separate but equal" and "states' rights" had become segregationist mantras and where the aspirations of blacks—especially their aspirations for their children—were rising as never before. African-American soldiers had returned from fighting freedom's war to find their children—and themselves—still oppressed in freedom's homeland. Black women, attuned as always to the deepest racial ironies of American life, were less willing than ever to see those ironies destroy their hopes for the future. And in the amazing burst of optimism and opportunity that followed the war, black children were learning that gradualism and compromise were not always the right answer, although courage might be.

As the desegregation train gathered momentum, more and more blacks (and more than a few whites as well) climbed aboard. Women, and even young girls, did so with particular enthusiasm and commitment, many inspired not only by their own deep yearnings but also by the memory of all the deeds of all the mothers, grandmothers, great-grandmothers, and great-great-grandmothers who went before them. Some of the pioneers, in fact, were still around, still setting examples. One of them was Mary Church Terrell.

A Symbol of Perseverance

It was fitting that Mrs. Terrell, born the year that Abraham Lincoln issued the Emancipation Proclamation, would live until two months after the *Brown* ruling. A teacher herself and a child of a former slave, she was a person of such indomitable will and clarity of vision that at least two generations of black women would extol and emulate her. Indeed, just a year before she died, "Mollie" Terrell, who had fought for women's suffrage and against lynching at the turn of the century; would celebrate, at ninety, a new civil rights victory of her own, when she completed the struggle that Pauli Murray and the Howard University students had begun almost a decade earlier at Thompson's cafeteria.

Mary Church Terrell's life is a tapestry of black American life, of blacks' perseverance and struggle, from Reconstruction to segregation. In 1881, the dazzling seventeen-year-old danced at President James Garfield's inaugural ball. Just a few years later, after the introduction of Jim Crow practices, Mary "Mollie" Church Terrell, now the college-educated wife of a successful black Washington lawyer, Robert Terrell, was manhandled on streetcars and turned away from restaurants and theaters she had once frequented. "As a colored woman," she wrote bitterly in 1940, "I may walk from the Capitol to the White House, ravenously hungry and abundantly supplied with money with which to purchase a meal, without finding a single restaurant in which I would be permitted to take a morsel of food."

Such treatment was particularly galling for a woman who was raised to believe she was as good as anybody else—and better than some. Her father was a former slave who had defied all the odds to become a millionaire real estate entrepreneur in Memphis. Mollie Church, from the age of six, was sent to white schools in Ohio. Fun-loving and popular, a nonstop talker, she was in perpetual motion and found it "extremely difficult . . . to keep still in school from the day I entered till I received my degree from college." She had many white friends but was quick to stand up for herself at the first sign of racism. When a teacher assigned her the role of a cowering black servant in a school play, young Mollie refused to take it.

Education and Travel

At Oberlin College, the first white college in the United States to admit blacks, she opted for the rigorous four-year Classical Course, including the study of Latin and Greek. Friends urged her to enroll instead in the "ladies'" Literary Course, which took only two years to complete. Too much education would harm her chances of getting a husband, they advised. "Where will you find a colored man who has studied Greek?" one friend asked her. Mollie ignored them and received her bachelor's degree in 1884.

Later, she studied French and German for two years in Europe, where several smitten young men, including a German baron, proposed marriage. As an old woman, Terrell would recall those lovestruck white youths as she tartly reflected on the widespread belief of whites that blacks were eager to marry them. "I am persuaded that the average Caucasian in this country believes that there is nothing which colored people desire so much as to marry into their group," she wrote. "It seems to me it is my duty to inform those who entertain this opinion that at least one colored woman voluntarily rejected such a proposition three times."

As one of the new genera-tion of independent, well-educated black women ac-tivists who came of age at the turn of the century, Mollie Church plunged into the fights for civil rights and women's rights. Her father

Mary Church Terrell

had wanted his headstrong daughter to be a "lady," like white women, and enjoy the luxury of staying at home and not working. But she considered that a "purposeless existence." Insisting on a life where "I could promote the welfare of my race," she went, instead, into teaching.

Terrell and Woman's Suffrage

From childhood, she had advocated the right to vote for women, once saying she could not "recall a period in my life . . . that I did not believe in woman's suffrage with all my heart." As a freshman at Oberlin, she wrote an essay called "Resolved, There Should Be a Sixteenth Amend-ment to the Constitution Granting Suffrage to Women." Though angered at white suffragists' lack of concern about black women, Terrell nonetheless worked closely with white leaders in the suffrage campaign. During World War I, she joined other suffragists in a months-long picket line in front of the White House. She was also active in efforts to improve living conditions for blacks. When the National Association of Colored Women was formed in 1896 to combat racial injustice and to organize social services for the black community, Terrell was elected its first president. In 1909, she signed the Call for creation of the NAACP and attended its organizing conference. Later, she was elected vice president of the organization's Washington branch.

The Aging Radical

Terrell was in her mid-eighties when World War II ended, and some regarded her as a throwback to a bygone era. Virginia Durr recalled that "Mrs. Terrell looked old and dressed old." But Terrell rejected the very idea that she might actually *be* old. "I can dance as long and as well as I ever did," she wrote at the age of seventy-seven, "although I get very few chances to do so." If there were any doubts about her strength and endurance, she put them to rest when she charged back into the public spotlight, more radical than ever, to lead an antisegregation battle in the nation's capital.

During Reconstruction, ordinances had been enacted to prohibit discrimination against blacks by restaurants, theaters, and other public places in the District of Columbia. Early in the post-Reconstruction era, when American-style apartheid was imposed, the city's white fathers didn't bother repealing the antidiscrimination laws; they simply ignored them. Segregation by fiat soon became as much a part of life in Washington as segregation by law in any city in the Deep South. Then, in 1946, the eighty-three-year-old Terrell was named head of an interracial committee demanding that the laws be enforced. She and the committee became the guiding force behind an extraordinary several-year campaign of picketing, leafleting, and boycotts. During a December snowstorm, the stooped, white-haired old lady, in her fur coat, gloves, and pearls, marched outside a downtown five-and-dime, one hand holding a "Don't Buy at Kresge's" placard, while, with the other hand, she leaned heavily on a cane. In the sweltering humidity of July, she was outside Hecht's department store, directing the action and inspiring her fellow marchers, among them a seven-year-old boy named Carl Bernstein and his mother. (Bernstein would later team with Bob Woodward at *The Washington Post* to help expose the Watergate cover-up.) "When my feet hurt," said another demonstrator, "I wasn't going to let a woman fifty years older than I do what I couldn't do. I kept on picketing." Said Eleanor Holmes Norton, a native Washingtonian who became a prominent figure in her own right in the civil rights struggle: "When I was a youngster, I didn't understand why black people were not protesting, had not found a way to protest. And then came Mary Church Terrell."

Challenging Segregation

On January 7, 1950, Terrell, accompanied by three companions, hobbled into Thompson's cafeteria near the White House, where Pauli Murray and the other Howard students had conducted their 1944 sit-in. Terrell got further than they did. She managed to place a bowl of soup on her tray before she and her friends were ordered to leave. That afternoon, their lawyers filed suit in a local court, alleging that Thompson's had broken the never-repealed Reconstruction laws. Three years later, the Supreme Court heard arguments in the Thompson's case, and on June 8, 1953, it handed down its decision: Racial segregation was against the law in Washington, D.C. "EAT ANYWHERE!" proclaimed a black Washington newspaper in a banner headline.

As immensely satisfying as the Supreme Court ruling was and as much as she delighted in the results of her long years of activism, Mary Church Terrell looked back on her life and thought wistfully about what might have been. At the age of seventy-seven, she had observed: "While I am grateful for the blessings which have been bestowed upon me and for the opportunities which have been offered, I cannot help wondering sometimes what I might have become and might have done if I had lived in a country which had not circumscribed and handicapped me on account of my race, but had allowed me to reach any height I was able to attain." Nothing that happened afterward, not even the victory in the Thompson's cafeteria case, changed her mind.

A teacher born during the Civil War, who lived to see the Supreme Court strike down "separate but equal" public education, might, however, have taken some satisfaction in the knowledge that her example, and that of many others like her, had helped to embolden a new generation of female activists.

Mary McLeod Bethune

Lerone Bennett Jr.

In 1896 the U.S. Supreme Court ruled in *Plessy v. Ferguson* that the "separate but equal" doctrine that bolstered racial segregation was constitutional. "Separate but equal" would shape American race relations for nearly sixty more years until *Plessy* was struck down by the Supreme Court in 1954 in its landmark *Brown v. Board of Education* decision. Indeed, while the original complaint in *Plessy* concerned segregated cars on a Louisiana train, the impact of the 1896 ruling struck all areas of black American life, not the least of which was public education. The handful of black colleges, which included Howard University, Mercer College, and Morehouse College, would remain inaccessible to most black youths, who were unable to obtain sound primary and secondary educations. Educational opportunities were especially limited for black girls. Determined to remedy the problem was activist-educator Mary McLeod Bethune (1875–1955), who founded the Daytona Literacy and Industrial School for Training Negro Girls in 1904 on a former garbage dump site in Daytona Beach, Florida. In 1923 the successful girls' school merged with the Cookman Institute for Men to become Bethune-Cookman College.

More than just an educator, Mary McLeod Bethune was also profoundly committed to the causes of black and

Lerone Bennett Jr., "Chronicles of Black Courage: Mary McLeod Bethune Started College with $1.50 and Faith," *Ebony*, vol. 57, February 2002. Copyright © 2002 by Lerone Bennett Jr. Reproduced by permission.

women's rights in general. The following profile by Lerone Bennett Jr. examines Bethune's courage and dedication, which led her to found the National Council of Negro Women and serve in the administration of President Franklin Delano Roosevelt.

The executive editor of *Ebony* magazine, Lerone Bennett Jr. is a widely published journalist and author. Among his many books on African American history are *Before the "Mayflower": A History of Black America, 1619–1962* and *What Manner of Man: A Biography of Martin Luther King Jr.*

☙   ☙   ☙

Courage comes in different packages and speaks different languages.

There is a courage called defiance, and there is a courage called perseverance.

There is a courage that shouts and a courage that whispers.

And although courage is generally identified with tumults and trumpets, it speaks loudest perhaps in small acts performed far from the applauding crowd—in the face of doubt, ridicule and disparagement—by a great spirit who refuses to give in or give up.

Such was the spirit of the young Mary McLeod Bethune, who was saved for immortality by the courage of the cotton field and the garbage dump. We know her best at the zenith of her career, when she advised presidents and shaped the vision of a whole generation of Black youths. But there can be no understanding of her character as it has passed into history without some understanding of the indomitable tenacity of spirit of the young woman who dreamed herself out of the cotton field and created a great restitution on a noxious dumping ground called "Hell's Hole."

In the course of a long and exemplary career, the great educator became a living legend and was listed among the 50 greatest women produced in America. But she maintained until the end that the road to the heights leads through a thicket of ordinary, even menial, tasks. "There is no menial work," she said once, "only menial spirits." The words she repeated on a thousand platforms became famous:

> Cease to be a drudge, seek to be an artist.

Daring to Dream

She was an artist, even in the cotton field. The daughter of former slaves and the sister of former slaves, born on July 10, 1875, near Mayesville, S.C., she was sent to the field at an early age and could pick 250 pounds of cotton by the time she was 9. But nothing—neither cotton nor drudger nor Jim Crow—dampened the spirit of young Mary Jane, who transcended her environment by refusing to be limited by the limits of her environment. Always everywhere, even in the cotton field, she dreamed dreams. She dreamed of books and light and a world where Black virtue and beauty would not be crushed by bales of whiteness.

"I knew then," she said later, "as I stood in the cotton field helping with the farm work that I was called to a task which I could not name or explain."

She knew it, but the Jim Crow laws of South Carolina did not know it. Unbelievable as it may seem in this age, when it is fashionable to decry the quality of Black schools, there were no schools for Blacks in Mayesville. Young Mary Jane was 11 when the Presbyterians opened a one-room mission school. She walked five miles a day to this school and completed the limited curriculum. She then returned to the cotton field, for there were no public high schools for Blacks in her area.

A lesser spirit would have been crushed by this setback, but in her case, as in so many other cases in Black history, defeat was a prelude, perhaps a necessary prelude, to victory. A White woman denoted a scholarship for a Black student "Who will make good." The local teacher remembered the light in the eyes of Mary McLeod, who went on to Scotia Seminary in North Carolina and Moody Bible Institute in Chicago. It was her intention then to go on to Africa as a missionary, but the eagerly awaited invitation never came, probably because of her race. Undaunted, the young woman returned to the South. She said later that she had wanted to go to Africa but what the Africa God called her to was named Florida.

In the years that followed, Mary McLeod taught school, married Albertus Bethune and gave birth to a son, Albert McLeod Bethune. Never for a moment, however, did she give up the great dream of her life—a school for Black girls. "I'd been dreaming," she said, "all my life, down yonder in the cotton fields, in the classroom, singing in the Chicago slums, dreaming, dreaming, of big buildings and little children—my own institution. But where to put it?"

The School in Daytona Beach

An answer came in 1904 when friends told her that there was a fertile missionary field in Daytona Beach, Florida, which was the focal point of a railroad construction project. Without a moment's hesitation, she caught a train for Daytona Beach and started her life's work. With capital of $1.50, raised by selling sandwiches and cakes to railroad construction workers, she rented a cottage and enrolled a handful of students. On October 4, 1904, the Daytona Literary and Industrial School for Training Negro Girls opened with five students.

Looking back later, Mrs. Bethune said:

We burned logs and used the charred splinters as pencils. For ink, we mashed up elderberries. Strangers gave us a broom, a lamp, some cretonne to drape around the ugly packing case which served as my first desk. Day after day, I went to the city dump and visited trash piles behind hotels, looking for discarded linen and kitchenware, cracked dishes and shattered chairs. I became adept at begging for bits of old lumber, bricks and even cement. Salvaging, reconstructing, and making bricks without straw were all part of our training.

To the surprise of doubters and detractors, the school prospered, and Mrs. Bethune looked around for an area of expansion. The only available spot was the city dump, an unsavory place called "Hell's Hole." The asking price was $250. By selling ice cream and pies to workers, Mrs. Bethune raised $5.00 and talked the owner into taking the balance over a two-year period.

With the help of students, parents and supportive Blacks, she cleared the dump and embarked on a frenzy of fund-raising. She sold sweet potato pies and fried fish. She sang at fashionable hotels, and she stood on street corners and begged.

People laughed at her. They called her a beggar and a dreamer. Undismayed by the ridicule and laughter, Mary McLeod Bethune went her way, and Blacks and Whites gathered under her banner. One day, so the story goes, a potential benefactor entered her office, which was furnished with crates and broken-down chairs.

"Where," asked the White philanthropist, "is this school you want me to be a trustee of?"

"In my mind," she answered, "and my soul."

Bethune's Lasting Legacy

With the help of powerful philanthropists, including James M. Gamble of Procter and Gamble, the institute grew into a secondary school and later, after a merger with Cookman Institute for Men, into a four-year college. When, in 1947, Mrs. Bethune relinquished the presidency, the institution was mortgage-free, had a faculty of 100 and a student enrollment of more than 1,000.

By this time, Mrs. Bethune was a national presence who defied the [Ku Klux] Klan and walked the Southland with the regal grace of the African rulers, from whom she said her mother descended. In later years she stumped the country against the poll tax, denounced lynching, and campaigned for wider social security coverage and a fair employment practices bill. She became a close friend of President Franklin D. Roosevelt and his wife, Eleanor Roosevelt. In 1935, she organized the National Council of Negro Women. In 1936 she was named director of the Negro Affairs Division of the National Youth Administration.

The great educator remained active until the end. When she died on May 17, 1955, after a full day of work at her desk, she was buried at her own request, on the college campus beneath the soil of the garbage dump she had transformed into a flower garden. Her "Last Will and Testament," one of the great documents of our history, was written exclusively for *EBONY* magazine shortly before her death. In it, she said:

- I leave you love. Love builds. It is positive and helpful. It is more beneficial than hate. Injuries quickly forgotten quickly pass away. Personally and racially, our enemies must be forgiven. Our aim must be to create a world of fellowship and justice where no man's skin color or religion is held against him. "Love thy neighbor" is a precept, which could transform the world if it were universally practiced. It connotes all human relations. Loving your neighbor means being interracial, interreligious and international.

- I leave you hope. The Negro's growth will be great in the years to come. Yesterday, our ancestors endured the degradation of slavery, yet they retained their dignity. Today, we direct our economic and political strength toward winning a more abundant and secure life. Tomorrow, a new Negro, unhindered by race taboos and shackles, will benefit from more than 330 years of ceaseless striving and struggle. Theirs will be a better world. This I believe with all my heart.

• I leave you the challenge of developing confidence in one another. As long as Negroes are hemmed into racial blocs by prejudice and pressure, it will be necessary for them to band together for economic betterment. Negro banks, insurance companies and other businesses are examples of successful, racial economic enterprises. These institutions were made possible by vision and mutual aid. Confidence was vital in getting them started and keeping them going. Negroes have got to demonstrate still more confidence in each other in business. This kind of confidence will aid the economic rise of the race by bringing together the pennies and dollars of our people and ploughing them into useful channels. Economic separatism cannot tolerate in this enlightened age, and it is not practicable. We must spread out as far and as fast as we can, but we must also help each other as we go.

• I leave you a thirst for education. Knowledge is the prime need of the hour. More and more, Negroes are taking full advantage of hard-won opportunities for learning, and the educational level of the Negro population is at its highest point in history. We are making greater use of the privileges inherent in living in a democracy. If we continue in this trend, we will be able to rear increasing numbers of strong, purposeful men and women, equipped with vision, mental clarity, health and education.

• I leave you a respect for the uses of power. We live in a world which respects power above all things. Power, intelligently directed, can lead to more freedom. Unwisely directed, it can be a dreadful, destructive force. During my lifetime I have seen the power of the Negro grow enormously. It has always been my first concern that this power should be placed on the side of human justice.

Now that the barriers are crumbling everywhere, the Negro in America must be ever vigilant lest his forces be marshaled behind wrong causes and undemocratic movements. He must not lend his support to any group that seeks to subvert democracy. That is why we must select leaders who are wise, courageous, and of great moral stature and ability. We have great leaders among us today. . . . We have had great men and women in the past: Frederick Douglass, Booker T. Washington, Harriet Tubman, Sojourner Truth, Mary Church Terrell. We must produce more qualified people like them, who will work not for themselves, but for others.

• I leave you faith. Faith is the first factor in life devoted to service. Without faith, nothing is possible. With it, nothing is impossible. Faith in God is the greatest power, but great, too, is faith in oneself. In 50 years the faith of the American Negro in himself has grown immensely and is still increasing. The measure of our progress as a race is in precise relation to the depth of the faith in our people held by our leaders. Frederick Douglass, genius though he was, was spurred by a deep conviction that his people would heed his counsel and follow him to freedom. Our greatest Negro figures have been imbued with faith. Our forefathers struggled for liberty in conditions far more onerous than those we now face, but they never lost the faith. Their perseverance paid rich dividends. We must never forget their sufferings and their sacrifices, for they were the foundations of the progress of our people.

• I leave you racial dignity. I want Negroes to maintain their human dignity at all costs. We, as Negroes, must recognize that we are the custodians as well as the heirs of a great civilization. We have given something to the world as a race and for this we are proud and fully conscious of our place in the total picture of mankind's development. We must learn also to share and mix with all men. We must make an effort to be less race conscious and more conscious of individual and human values. I have never been sensitive about my complexion. My color has never destroyed my self-respect nor has it ever caused me to conduct myself in such a manner as to merit the disrespect of any person. I have not let my color handicap me. Despite many crushing burdens and handicaps, I have risen from the cotton fields of South Carolina to found a college, administer it during its years of growth, become a public servant in the government of our country and a leader of women. I would not exchange my color for all the wealth in the world, for had I been born White I might not have been able to do all that I have done. . . .

• I leave you a desire to live harmoniously with your fellow men. The problem of color is worldwide. It is found in Africa and Asia, Europe and South America. I appeal to American Negroes—North, South, East and West—to recognize their common problems and unite to solve them.

I pray that we will learn to live harmoniously with the White race. So often, our difficulties have made us hyper-sensitive and truculent. I want to see my people conduct themselves naturally in all relationships—fully conscious of their manly responsibilities and deeply aware of their heritage. I want them to learn to understand Whites and influence them for good, for it is advisable and sensible for us to do so. We are a minority . . . living side by side with a White majority. We must learn to deal with these people positively and on an individual basis.

• I leave you finally a responsibility to our young people. The world around us really belongs to youth for youth will take over its future management. Our children must never lose their zeal for building a better world. They must not be discouraged from aspiring toward greatness, for they are to be the leaders of tomorrow. Nor must they forget that the masses of our people are still underprivileged, ill-housed, impoverished and victimized by discrimination. We have a powerful potential in our youth, and we must have the courage to change old ideas and practices so that we may direct the power toward good ends.

Faith, courage, brotherhood, dignity, ambition, responsibility—these are needed today as never before. We must cultivate them and use them as tools for our task of completing the establishment of equality for the Negro. We must sharpen these tools in the struggle that faces us and find new ways of using them. The Freedom Gates are half ajar. We must pry them fully open.

If I have a legacy to leave my people—it is my philosophy of living and serving. I pray now that my philosophy may be helpful to those who share my vision of a world of Peace, Progress, Brotherhood and Love.

Doors Closed to Black Americans

Mary McLeod Bethune

In the following speech delivered at Bethune-Cookman College in 1936, Mary McLeod Bethune addresses the widespread discrimination that precludes black Americans from partaking in the rights of citizenship. Likening the plight of blacks to that of handicapped individuals, Bethune calls on the nation to extend its ostensible core principle of justice to all Americans and throw open the doors currently closed by segregation and unequal treatment.

❦   ❦   ❦

Frequently from some fair-minded speaker who wishes his platform utterances to fall on pleased ears, comes this expression: "Do not continually emphasize the fact that you are a Negro, forget that," and quite as frequently there is always the desire to hurl back this challenge, "You be a Negro for just one short twenty-four hours and see what your reaction will be." A thousand times during that twenty-four hours, without a single word being said, he would be reminded and

Mary McLeod Bethune, speech delivered at Bethune-Cookman College, Daytona Beach, Florida, 1936.

would realize unmistakably that he is a Negro.

These are some of the experiences he would have that would be exactly as mine often are: One morning I started to catch a train. There was plenty of time to make the train with ease. Although several taxi-cabs passed as I stood on the corner trying to hail one, several minutes passed before one would stop to serve me, and so caused me to be three minutes late in catching that train.

On another occasion with time to spare, with sufficient money in my pocket to have every comfort that was necessary, I found that I was compelled to take a "jim crow" car in order to reach my destination in Mississippi. As a passenger on that "jim crow" car there was no service that I could receive in securing a meal, although from every other coach accommodations could be had.

Choices Limited by Prejudice

When last winter a number of Negro women were discussing where their respective children should attend school, they were [limited to the consideration] of Negro schools exclusively, since they were all members of a southern community. Then as they thought of further education for their children they were again limited to those institutions which will accept a limited number of Negro students. Some little while ago one of the best lecturers in this country was giving a lecture at the close of the Mid-week religious service, and there again, although the services and the lecturer appealed to me, there was no way that I could, with any sense of self-respect, enter when I realized the segregation and separation that awaited me on that occasion.

Not only the cultural avenues, but the economic fields are closed also. My boy belonged to a labor union, but when there came the chance for the distribution of jobs, it was not until all white applicants had been supplied, and then even though he is a skilled laborer, nothing was offered him in his own field, but he was forced to accept a job as a common laborer.

The white-collar jobs are largely closed to the majority of Negroes, although they have given themselves to the making of this country. The very forests that the Negroes have turned into fertile fields are often not open to them.

As I walked down the street, passing restaurants, cafes, hotels, not necessarily with blazing, glaring signs, but with a subtle determination there is the expression "no admittance."

The "Handicap" of Race

Whether it be my religion, my aesthetic taste, my economic opportunity, my educational desire, whatever the craving is, I find a limitation because I suffer the greatest known handicap, a Negro—a Negro woman.

As the director—mother of the next generation guiding the Negro youth of this land, the citizenry who must share the responsibility of this country, whatever it is, I find that the Negro youth cannot have, and enjoy, the highest places of citizenship, but must measure up to that standard, nevertheless. As a part of the citizenry of this country, the greatest country in all the world, he is expected to be a superior being despite the ever-increasing limitations. The outstanding Negro has proportionately more than met this requirement in the fields of letters, music, economics, and research education, in fact, in every line of endeavor.

The doors in almost every field—political, educational, economical, and social—are closed, barred against him, but they must be opened. Shall it be a question whether or not the Negro, himself, will batter down the doors; whether or not the government will open some of them for him; whether or not the fair-mindedness of the country shall force them to open is a question. But they must be opened if the Negro is to live up to, and attain, unto his best.

The Rights of Citizenship

Theoretically, to be an American citizen implies that every American citizen shall have life, liberty, and pursuit of happiness without anyone else's let [permission] or hindrance. Yet, these rules do not apply equally to the Negro as [they do] to the white man. There are very many doors that are shut against the Negro, but all of these are not barred. They may be opened with tact, skill, and persistence.

The first privilege of a citizen is to be well-born. The day of the midwife is largely passed, and the expectant mother should have the best care of physician and hospital. Many children are handicapped for life by not having had the proper medical attention preceding birth, at birth, and immediately following birth. Even then there is general medical assistance along these lines for white people, [t]he door is generally shut to the Negro. In many places, if he is taken into the hospital at all, he is taken into the cellar or some isolated corner and given scarce attention by unwilling hands. The necessary food for mother and child is often beyond the reach of such persons, not only because of color only. These handicaps follow child and adult in the Southland and are often present in the Northland, where equality, on the surface, is pretended.

Next to birth and life itself come housing and sanitary conditions. The Negro sections of most southern towns are just across the railroad where there are neither paved streets, under drainage, nor sufficient lighting. Nor are there rules of health that compel those who occupy these sections to observe the most common rules of sanitation. The Federal Housing and Community Bills have not gone far enough to penetrate across the railroad where the people who most need them may be accommodated. And even in the North and more liberal communities the Negro often finds himself in the old, and often abandoned part of the community, where the better class of white people have left to move into up-to-date, better ventilated, better heated, and better constructed homes.

The child handicapped at birth for want of proper medical and home surroundings most often finds that his school facilities are both very limited and very poor. The school houses, if such they may be called, are poorly constructed and lighted, and have straight-back benches with seats often too high for small children, or too small for older pupils, neither properly lighted nor properly heated. When the parents are too poor to buy suitable books, no provisions are made for buying them. In many places there is an attempt to segregate colored taxation to colored schools, which means the white child gets ten months of schooling under favorable conditions while the colored child gets four or five months with very poor facilities, and poorly educated and equally poorly paid teachers. These conditions make it very easy for the Negro in later years to "knock and not be heard." The Negro is expected to be a citizen and obey all laws which he often has no facilities for knowing and certainly no opportunity for making.

Segregation and Discrimination

It is notorious that the Negro is deprived of his civil rights in public places. He has no opportunity to contact the white community in those things which make for right living, worthwhile accomplishments, and high citizenship. The cultural advantages of the concert, lectures, and public discussions are closed to him. He is further handicapped by not being able to work at the ordinary trades controlled by labor unions. It matters not what a Negro's qualifications are, it is difficult for him to become a member of a united labor organization, and to function as a member of the AFL [American Federation of Labor]. These labor organizations control most of the worthwhile employment and scrupulously exclude the Negro from membership and even where the Negro is permitted to join he is given the most menial work, and the least paying jobs.

Mary McLeod Bethune

In railroad travel the Negro is segregated in the South and made to ride in filthy, dingy, unsanitary cars. At the railroad station there is some kind of a toilet facility marked "colored." But even these facilities are denied those who by virtue of their economic conditions are forced to ride in buses. These bus lines often have only one set of toilet accommodations for men and for women which means white men and women. The colored passenger who often has to shift for himself, has to go to a nearby house or go to the woods and bushes in order to get an opportunity for the proper evacuations. Then too, when he enters the buses, he is assigned to the seats over the wheels where he is both cramped and jolted.

A colored man may be a fireman on a southern train, and may know all about how to run the engine, but if the engineer gets sick or dies, a white man must be sent for to move the train off the tracks into the barn. The labor union forbids him to join the union or place his hand on the throttle.

In states in which the State Board controls the sale of

liquor, such as Pennsylvania, a colored man is not permitted to be a salesman, but [permitted to be] a janitor or truck driver. And although the government will furnish him money by way of relief to buy the liquor, the government will not see that he has a chance to earn a living for his wife and family through dispensing the liquor.

In the armed branch of the government the Negro can be little more than common fodder. In the Navy it matters not what his qualifications may be, he can rise no higher than a mess boy; and the same thing is generally true of the Army. The once vaulted 9th and 10th Cavalries and the 24th and 25th Infantries have virtually been abolished to the colored man and he can only be a cleaner in that branch of the government. But in case of actual war, he is conscripted and sent to the front as shock troops. This prejudiced viewpoint on behalf of the government not only deprives colored men of the privilege of playing soldier, but also prevents them and their families from getting what could come to them through wages.

Black Contributions to the Nation

Beginning as the Negro did with the founding of the colonies, contributing as he has to every phase of American life, he should have the same rights, privileges, immunities, and emoluments that have been and are accorded to any American citizen, and the government standing *in loco parentis* should neither make nor allow any discriminations or differences in any of her citizens, and should go a step further and see that no citizen, group of citizens, municipal or state government treat the Negro differently from all other citizens. That means that in the positions of responsibility, honor and trust, without . . . the right to earn a living at any trade or occupation for which he is qualified, the government should see to it that the Negro is not barred therefrom.

The Negro wants a fair chance to work out his own destiny and to continue to contribute to the honor and glory of the nation. But this is impossible if he is to be handicapped, circumscribed, separated, and segregated.

The Negro wants equality of opportunity. He asks the privilege of entering every door and avenue that he may be able to prove his value. The Negro asks: "Can America, the land of the free, continue to refuse to answer this knock at these now closed doors; to refuse to grant him these quested opportunities of equality whereby he will make a finer, higher and more acceptable citizen?" The Negro must go to a separate church even though he claims to be of the same denomination [as some whites]. He is not allowed to sing, in unison with the white man, the grand old hymns of Calvin, the Wesleys—the triumphant songs of Christ and eternal glory.

When at last he is called to his final resting place on earth, even his ashes are not allowed to mingle with those of his white brother, but are borne away to some remote place where the white man is not even reminded that this Negro ever lived.

Judging from all that has preceded the Negro in death, it looks as if he has been prepared for a heaven, separate from the one to which the white man feels he alone is fit to inhabit.

Thus in death and for eternity, as in life, the white man would see the Negro segregated.

Justice Demands Equality

The rankest injustice is meted out to the Negro when he has helped in every way the development of the country, and yet finds that he is not permitted to share fully and freely in that development.

The principle of justice is fundamental and must be exercised if the peoples of this country are to rise to the highest and best, for there can be neither freedom, peace, true democracy, or real development without justice. The closed door of economic inequalities, of educational limitation, of social restrictions comprise the greatest injustice possible. None need fear the change for which we plead. The door of opportunity with all its ramifications, leading into every avenue, can be opened without this evolution causing revolution. This is a high challenge to America—to the church—and to the state. Just now there seems to be an effort on the part of our great leader [Franklin D. Roosevelt], the President of the United States, to open for the Negro some of the doors that have been closed. Too, there is a determination on the part of the Negro to open, or batter down, some of these closed doors. But more, there must be an equal plan or cooperation on the part of the American public to join in the effort. How will this challenge be met?

It seems to me that here is his challenge to America. Can it—will it? If it further closes the door of opportunity to a part of its own citizenry, it will be guilty of the very outrage that led to its own founding.

Awake America! Accept the challenge! Give the Negro a chance!

Rosa Parks

Gregory J. Reed

Rosa Parks (1913–) is considered by many to be the mother of the modern civil rights movement. Her refusal to surrender her bus seat to a white man on December 1, 1955, in Montgomery, Alabama, an act of defiance for which she was arrested and jailed, prompted 381 days of boycotts that ultimately resulted in the desegregation of the Montgomery bus system and other public facilities. Despite the mainstream media's tendency to portray Parks as a simple, apolitical housewife, in truth she had been active in the NAACP and voter registration drives well in advance of the pivotal events on that Thursday evening in 1955 that made her, along with Martin Luther King Jr., one of the most celebrated figures in the fight for black rights. The following selection by Gregory J. Reed provides an overview of Parks's life and her contributions to the cause of black equality. Gregory J. Reed, attorney, author, and editor, cofounded the Parks Legacy with Rosa Parks.

Rosa Parks was born Rosa Louise McCauley on February 4, 1913, in Tuskegee, Alabama. Named after her maternal grandmother, Rosa was the first child of

James and Leona (Edwards) McCauley. James was a carpenter and a builder. Leona was a teacher. When Rosa was still a toddler, James decided to go north in search of work. Leona, who was pregnant with Rosa's brother by then, wanted a stable home life for her children. She and Rosa moved in with her parents, Sylvester and Rose, in Pine Level, Alabama. Rosa saw her father again briefly when she was five years old, and after that did not see him until she was grown and married.

Though Rosa longed to go to school, chronic illnesses kept her from attending regularly in her early years. Her mother taught her at home, and nurtured Rosa's love of books and learning. The schools for black children in Pine Level didn't go beyond the sixth grade, so when Rosa completed her education in Pine Level at age 11, her mother enrolled her in the Montgomery Industrial School for Girls (also known as Miss White's School for Girls), a private school for African American girls. Several years later Rosa went on to Alabama State Teachers' College for Negroes, which had a program for black high school students in training to be teachers. When Rosa was 16, her grandmother became ill. Rosa left school to help care for her. Her grandmother Rose died about a month later. As Rosa prepared to return to Alabama State, her mother also became ill. Rosa decided to stay home and care for her mother, while her brother, Sylvester, worked to help support the family.

The Parks's Early Activism

Rosa married Raymond Parks in December 1932. Raymond was born in Wedowee, Alabama, in 1903. Like Rosa's mother, Leona McCauley, Geri Parks encouraged her son's love of education. Even though he received little formal education, Raymond overcame the confines of racial segregation and educated himself. His thorough knowledge of domestic affairs and current events led most people to believe he had gone to college.

Raymond supported Rosa's dream of completing her formal education, and in 1934 Rosa received her high school diploma. She was 21 years old. After she received her diploma, she worked in a hospital and took in sewing before getting a job at Maxwell Field, Montgomery's Army Air Force base.

Raymond was an early activist in the effort to free the Scottsboro Boys, nine young African American men who were falsely accused of raping two white women, and he stayed involved in the case until the last defendant was released on parole in 1950. In their early married years, Raymond and Rosa worked together in the National Association for the Advancement of Colored People (NAACP). In 1943 Rosa became secretary of the NAACP, and later served as a youth leader.

Parks's refusal to give up her bus seat to a white man in 1955 prompted a boycott that resulted in the desegregation of the Montgomery bus system.

It was also in 1943 that Rosa tried to register to vote. She tried twice before being told that she didn't pass the required test. That year Rosa was put off a Montgomery city bus for boarding in the front rather than in the back, as was the rule for African American riders.

She tried again in 1945 to register to vote. This time she copied the questions and her answers by hand so she could prove later she had passed. But this time she received her voter's certificate in the mail.

The Turning Point

In August of 1955, Rosa met the Reverend Martin Luther King, Jr., at an NAACP meeting, where he was a guest speaker. Some months later, Rosa was busy organizing a workshop for an NAACP youth conference. On the evening of December 1, 1955, Rosa finished work and boarded the bus to go home. She noticed that the driver was the same man who had put her off the bus twelve years earlier. Black people were supposed to ride in the back of the bus. Rosa took a seat in the middle.

Soon the bus became crowded with passengers. The "white" seats filled up. A white man was left standing. Tired of giving in to injustice, Rosa refused to surrender her seat on the bus. Two policemen came and arrested her.

Rosa's act of quiet courage changed the course of history.

The Impact of the Boycotts

Four days later, the black people of Montgomery and sympathizers of other races organized and announced a boycott of the city bus line. Known as the Montgomery Bus Boycott, this protest lasted for 381 days. During this time, African Americans walked or arranged for rides rather than take the bus. Reverend King, the spokesperson for the boycott, urged participants to protest nonviolently. Soon the protest against racial injustice spread beyond Montgomery and throughout the country. The modern-day Civil Rights movement in America was born.

The bus boycott ended on December 21, 1956, after the U.S. Supreme Court declared bus segregation in Montgomery unconstitutional on November 13. Not long afterward, Rosa and Raymond, who had endured threatening telephone calls and other harassments during the boycott, moved to Detroit.

After Montgomery

Rosa remained active in the Civil Rights movement. She traveled, spoke, and participated in peaceful demonstrations. From 1965 to 1988, she worked in the office of Congressman John Conyers of Michigan. During those years, Rosa endured the assassination of Dr. Martin Luther King, Jr., in 1968 and she suffered the deaths of her husband and brother in 1977 and her mother in 1979.

Rosa's interest in working with young people stayed strong, and in 1987 she co-founded the Rosa and Raymond Parks Institute for Self-Development for the purpose of motivating young people to achieve their highest potential. In the years since her arrest, Rosa Parks has been recognized throughout America as the mother of the modern-day Civil Rights movement. For children and adults, Mrs. Parks is a role model for courage, an example of dignity and determination. She is a symbol of freedom for the world.

In 1995 Mrs. Parks joined children and adults all over the world to mark the 40th anniversary of the Montgomery Bus Boycott, through marches, lectures, exhibits, and many other events. She co-founded a new organization, The Parks Legacy. A movement among legislators was launched to establish February 4, Mrs. Parks' birthday, as a national legal holiday.

Profiles · in · History

Voting Rights, Women's Rights, and Speaking for the Voiceless

Fannie Lou Hamer

Chana Kai Lee

Fannie Lou Hamer (1917–1977) was among the most in-
spirational activists of the civil rights movement. Perhaps
best known for proclaiming, "I'm sick and tired of being
sick and tired," Hamer endured harassment, humiliation,
and physical brutality in her quest to exercise her right to
vote and ensure that other southern blacks be able to do
the same. A gifted grassroots organizer and a powerful
public speaker, Hamer was instrumental in the formation
of the Mississippi Freedom Democratic Party that went on
to challenge (albeit unsuccessfully) the racist exclusivity of
the state's delegation at the 1964 Democratic National
Convention. Although the convention challenge was in
vain, Hamer's passionate speech before the Credentials
Committee, which was televised across the nation, helped
lay the groundwork for the 1965 passage of the Voting
Rights Act by Congress. The following selection by Chana
Kai Lee serves as a preface to her book-length study of
Hamer's life and her impact on the civil rights movement.

Chana Kai Lee, associate professor of history and
women's studies at the University of Georgia, is author of
For Freedom's Sake: The Life of Fannie Lou Hamer and the
senior editor of *The Encyclopedia of Women in World History*.

🐝 🐝 🐝

Chana Kai Lee, *For Freedom's Sake: The Life of Fannie Lou Hamer*. Chicago: University of Illinois Press, 1999. Copyright © 1999 by the Board of Trustees of the
University of Illinois. Reproduced by permission.

Biographies of the poor make generous offerings. They teach us just as much about the empowered as they do about the dispossessed and disfranchised. Life histories of the privileged are rarely as kind. Invariably, a humbling possibility grabs our attention: on some abstract, symbolic level, oppressed individuals ultimately *can so* reclaim value and garner just rewards from their historic battles against devaluation and exclusion. After all, it is what they have done and said during the fight that warrants our writing about them. In this sense and others, the meaning and consequences of a poor person's life stretch far beyond the scope of that life, and far beyond the limits that others had set for it. It makes sense, then, that a poor woman's story—a poor, black southern woman's story—could speak so thoroughly to a central theme of American history: the fight for political and economic freedom.

This is such a story. It is one account of the life and times of the civil rights activist Fannie Lou Hamer. It is at once the story of a major social protest movement and of a remarkably dedicated black woman from the Mississippi Delta. The last of twenty children born into a sharecropping family, Hamer drew strength and inspiration from poverty and racism and went on to become one of the most respected leaders of her day.

The Impact of Early Influences

Early influences on Hamer's character were everlasting. A bold and attentive mother shaped Hamer's understanding of race, class, work, and sex in the South. Through her mother's words and actions, Hamer came to appreciate the individual power that flowed from clever, self-affirming responses to injustice. Psychologically, she had to, for vulnerability was an onerous reality for black girls and women in the Jim Crow South.

Unquestionably, Hamer's identity was also shaped by sexualized racial violence—her grandmother's rape, which Hamer learned of as a girl, and the involuntary sterilization and sexual molestation that Hamer experienced as an adult. These experiences took up meaningful space in her inner life; the agony and anger were constant. In addition, beginning as early as age six, Hamer led a hard, uncertain existence as an exploited sharecropper. For much of her life, deprivation defined her material existence.

Joining the Fight for Equality

The summer of 1962 marked her formal entry into the civil rights movement. Arrests, bombings, and job dismissals followed, but Hamer continued working as a field secretary with the Student Nonviolent Coordinating Committee (SNCC) throughout the early sixties. She conducted door-to-door canvassing and taught citizenship classes throughout the rural South. As a dynamic speaker and moving singer, Hamer also contributed significantly to the organization's fund-raising. Through her work with SNCC and the Mississippi Freedom Democratic Party (MFDP), an organization she cofounded, Hamer helped bring thousands of blacks into an institutionalized political process, an important step in African Americans' quest for improving life-chances.

Among her many contributions, Hamer is remembered most for the stand she made at the 1964 Democratic National Convention in New Jersey. There, Hamer led an MFDP challenge to unseat the all-white Mississippi delegation. The highlight of the convention came when Hamer delivered a passionate account of the 1963 police beating in Winona, Mississippi, that left her partially blind. It was at this point that Hamer rose to national prominence.

Beginning in 1965, Hamer began concentrating her efforts on economic self-reliance through the Mississippi Freedom Labor Union, Head Start programs, and the Freedom Farm Corporation, a cooperative venture she established to feed, clothe, and house Mississippi's poor. In many ways, the building of the corporation was largely a one-woman effort. Hamer traveled thousands of miles to raise funds for the farm, making numerous speeches and conducting intensive letter-writing campaigns. Thousands of people were fed and clothed in Sunflower County, and similar projects sprang up in surrounding areas. Throughout the 1970s, Hamer combined all of her strategies for change—she ran for office, participated in party conventions, boycotted stores, initiated school desegregation law suits, and spoke out on the lead issues of her time, from the Vietnam War to abortion.

The Significance of Race, Sex, and Class

Accounting for her actions and reactions, both political and personal, demands recognition of the shifting social contexts for Hamer's life. These contexts gained meaning from the general configuration of race, sex, and class hierarchies of Hamer's time and place, and from the relative positioning of Hamer in her various social settings. As a worker, Hamer spent most of her adult life as a destitute farmer charged with supervising others and keeping records for the plantation. In her marriage, Hamer was a take-charge woman who never allowed her civil rights activities to be circumscribed by the demands of family and marriage, a fact that she kept private—apparently because of her conflicting feelings concerning what participation in the movement meant for her marriage. In her public life, Hamer was the outspoken, indignant grass-roots leader who was highly respected and sometimes even feared. Most people in the civil rights movement respected her leadership largely because, in her public persona, she was the quintessential victim of racism and poverty who chose to stand tall and unbroken in the face of ever-present defeat. Yet, it was this same position that was partly responsible for keeping her outside the circle of mainstream, middle-class, "more respectable" civil rights leaders, many of whom regarded her plainspoken, abrasive manner as too much of an embarrassment in the real world of politics. Combined, these roles represented a curious sort of status for Hamer the wife, mother, farm worker, and political activist. They created a duality of being that, on one hand, allowed her much leverage and influence but, on the other hand, often left her angry, unfulfilled, wanting, and confused. As a plantation timekeeper, grassroots leader, and self-directed mother and wife, Hamer assumed positions that became their own sources of authority for her, sources that occasionally allowed her small doses of agency in her political and private worlds.

Fannie Lou Hamer

Struggles and Triumphs

Although personal tragedy and political disappointment were constant, Hamer's life is not a story of complete victimization or defeat. Neither is it an example of complete triumph over all odds. The impact of her experiences falls somewhere in between. Her civil rights struggles brought many rewards, but they also resulted in enormous personal pain, disappointment, and exhaustion. In the end, after movement activity had waned and the national attention had discovered a new focus, she was left virtually alone to assess the consequences of her sacrifices made in a quest for freedom. This book is as much about the collective journey as about the personal costs.

Hamer was just one of a number of black women leaders in the civil rights movement. Black women played pivotal roles in every significant stage of the movement. It was Daisy Bates who led the 1957 challenge to desegregate the all-white Central High School in Little Rock, Arkansas. Septima Clark, a longtime educator, engineered the first citizenship schools, which encouraged and trained local leaders throughout the South. Moreover, had it not been for Ella Baker, a veteran activist, the youthful energy of the movement might never have found the effective organizational base that SNCC provided. Black women afforded the civil rights movement a style of leadership that contributed greatly to its success, and it was the destitute sharecropper Fannie Lou Hamer who rose up and gave this style of leadership its broadest appeal.

Through her leadership, Fannie Lou Hamer represented a necessary left-wing tendency within the civil rights movement. She functioned as both symbol and worker. She was truly one of those well-respected individuals in the movement who walked others through rough times by mere example and by actual hands-on help. To many, she was one of those "mamas" in the movement. According to Charles Sherrod, a SNCC member, "the 'mamas' were usually the militant women in the community—outspoken, understanding, and willing to catch hell, having already caught their share." This study is an effort to document the life experience of one of those women, a woman whose share of hell was undeniably convincing testament to the power of the human spirit.

A Life Shaped by Mentors: Marian Wright Edelman

Marian Wright Edelman

Marian Wright Edelman (1939–), a Yale-educated lawyer, author, and veteran of the civil rights movement, is the foremost children's advocate in the United States. In 1973 Edelman founded the Children's Defense Fund, a private nonprofit organization that lobbies for the interests of disadvantaged children, including health care, education, and preschool and after-school programs. Stressing the importance of black self-help and community, the Children's Defense Fund, with Edelman at the helm, is dedicated to speaking for those without a political voice, the nation's poor children. In the following selection excerpted from the preface to her book *Lanterns: A Memoir of Mentors*, Edelman recounts the profound influence of family, friends, teachers, and heroes from both the past and the present on her lifelong commitment to racial, social, and economic justice.

❦ ❦ ❦

It is my great joy to share some of the great lives and spirits of mentors who have enriched, informed, and helped shape my life. Many of them helped shape our times and national life.

I was born in the sturdy white wood parsonage at 119 Cheraw Street in Bennettsville, South Carolina, as the last of five children of Rev. Arthur Jerome and Maggie Leola Bowen Wright. My birth house is now a Children's Defense Fund office.

I have always felt blessed to be born who I was, where I was, when I was, and with the parents I had. As a Black girl child growing up in a small segregated southern town, I could never take anything for granted and never for a moment lacked a purpose worth fighting, living, and dying for, or an opportunity to make a difference if I wanted to. I was richly blessed with parents and community elders who nurtured me and other children and tried to live what they preached. They believed in God, in family, in education, and in helping others.

I did not come into or get through life alone. Neither did you. Our mothers had to push to get us here. And our fathers had to help too. My parents needed and got help in raising me and my sister and three brothers from our neighbors and friends in their church and community, some of whom you will meet here. They tried unceasingly to protect children from the unfair assaults of southern racial segregation and injustice by weaving a tight family and community fabric of love around us. . . .

Everyday Heroes and Influences

This book is about the crucial influences of the *natural daily* mentors in my life—my parents, community co-parents and elders, preachers, teachers, civic and civil rights leaders. It is about the impact of cultural, social, economic, and political forces that created the external context within which my family and Black community elders lived, and about how they influenced and shaped my perceptions and life choices. The challenge faced by Black parents when I was growing up was daunting. They had to affirm and help us children internalize our sanctity as children of God, as valued members of our family, of the Black community, of the American community, and of the entire human community, while simultaneously preparing us to understand, survive in, and challenge the prevailing values of a legally segregated nation, with a history of slavery, that did not value or affirm us as equal citizens or practice the self-evident belief that "all men are created equal" as its founding fathers professed.

Black parents—and all parents—face these same challenges today to help children define who they are and what to value in a culture that assigns worth more by extrinsic than intrinsic measures; by racial, gender, and class rather than human values; by material rather than spiritual values; by power rather than principle; by money rather than morality; by greed rather than goodness; by consumerism rather than conscience; by rugged individualism rather than community; and that glorifies violence above nonviolence.

I cannot recall a single one of the mentors I share with you in this book ever talking to me just about how to make a living or to get a job—worthy and necessary goals. They all stressed how to make a life and to find a purpose worth living for and to leave the world better than I found it. Their emphasis was on education, excellence, and service—not just on career. Their message was that if I were excellent I'd have less trouble securing a job—even as a young Black person. I can't remember the clothes a single one of them wore or the kind of car they drove or whether they drove a car at all.

What I do remember is their integrity, courage in the face of adversity, perseverance, and shared passion for justice and a better life for children—their own and other people's—and for education as a means to the end of helping others. With one exception, Charles E. Merrill, Jr., son of the scion of the Merrill Lynch brokerage firm, none had much money. Some of them had none and lived hand-to-mouth by the grace of God and friends. And Charles Merrill knew that money was a means to help others and not an end. He used his to give dozens of young women and men like me and [black writer and activist] Alice Walker a chance to travel and study abroad and to experience the world he had been privileged to see.

The Education Born of Experience
Many of my mentors were well educated but many did not have much or any formal education. However they valued education for their children and were very astute about life. Some of the wisest words I have heard and most important lessons I have learned did not come from Harvard or Yale or Princeton or law school or Ph.D. trained mouths. They came from poor women and men educated in the school of life. Their books were struggle. Their pencils and pens were sharpened by poverty. Their mother wit was created by the daily battle for survival. Their inner faith was nourished by their outer losses. Their eyes were riveted on searching for and doing God's will rather than human ways, and their standards were divine rather than human justice.

I have always wanted to be half as good, half as brave, and half as faithful as the great women of my childhood and young adulthood like Miz Tee, Miz Lucy, Miz Kate, Mrs. Fannie Lou Hamer, and Mrs. Mae Bertha Carter [Hamer and Carter were civil rights activists], whom I introduce here. They represent countless unsung lives

of grace, women who carry on day-in and day-out trying to keep their families, churches, and communities
together and to instill by example the enduring values of
love, hard work, discipline, and courage.

When Miss Osceola McCarthy, an elderly Mississippi woman who washed and ironed White folks'
clothes all her life, gained national prominence after
giving a large portion ($150,000) of her life's savings to
the University of Southern Mississippi to provide
scholarships for young Blacks to enter the doors that
had been closed to her, many people were amazed. I
was not. In less dramatic ways, I have seen many such
role models who worked hard, earned more than they
thought they needed to live on, and saved the rest to
share with others.

I think about them when I read about young Wall
Street executives complaining about the difficulties of
maintaining a "decent lifestyle" on their million-dollar
salaries and bonuses. I think about Mrs. Hamer and
Mrs. Carter when I hear young Black, Brown, and
White people whine about how hard life is. They don't
know from hard as they excuse themselves from trying
and decide to give up after the first, second, fifth, or
tenth failure, or dissolve into despair or lash out at others when somebody hurts their feelings or insults them.
Every time I am tempted (as is often) to give up or excuse myself from "doing one more thing," I think of
Miz Mae Bertha or Miz Fannie Lou who until they
died called up regularly to discuss how to solve some
problem they could have conveniently ignored. Their
examples make me stand up when I want to sit down,
try one more time when I want to stop, and go out the
door when I want to stay home and relax.

From the beginning, I was surrounded by strong
Black female role models from my mother to Miz Tee,
Miz Lucy, and Miz Kate and other community women,

to Ella Baker during my college years, to the great women of Mississippi. Black women were steady anchors who helped me navigate every step of my way through childhood, college, law school, and as I tested adult professional wings. All of my mentors encouraged me by word or example to think and act outside the box and to ignore the low expectations many have for Black girls and women.

Mentors Transcend Race, Color, and Creed

My mentors came in both genders, and in different colors, faiths, and persuasions. Three Black men, my daddy, Morehouse College president Benjamin E. Mays, and his mentee Dr. Martin Luther King, Jr., and three White men, Morehouse College board chair Charles E. Merrill, Jr., my college professor, historian Howard Zinn, and former Yale chaplain, William Sloane Coffin, Jr., played pivotal roles at key points in my life. What they all had in common was their respectful treatment of me as an important, thinking individual human being. They expressed no sense of limits on my potential or on who they thought I could become, and they engaged me as a fellow wayfarer and struggler. They saw me inside and not just outside and affirmed the strengths I had *because* I was blessed to be born a Black girl child.

All of my mentors, men and women of different faiths and colors, in their own way personified excellence and courage, shared and instilled a vision and hope of what could be, not what was, in our racially, gender, class, and caste constricted country; kept America's promise of becoming a country free of discrimination, poverty, and ignorance ever before me; put the foundations of education, discipline, hard work, and perseverance needed to help build it beneath me; and instilled a sense of the here and now and forever faithful presence of God inside me.

In the *Odyssey*, Homer used the name Mentor for an old and faithful friend of King Odysseus. The goddess Athena impersonates Mentor to inspire and impart wisdom and encouragement to prepare Odysseus' son Telemachus for his journey in search of his father, saying: "You will not lack either courage or sense in the future." Neither the king nor his son knew where their quests would lead them or what they would find.

A Life's Journey Comes Full Circle

I look back in wonder and gratitude at my rich uncharted journey from my small hometown of Bennettsville, South Carolina, to cloistered Spelman College in Atlanta, Georgia in a segregated South, through Europe and the Soviet Union for fifteen months, back to Spelman and a changing South, into the southern Civil Rights Movement, through Yale Law School and into the north of America with its subtler but persistent racial codes, to Mississippi as a civil rights lawyer, to Washington, D.C. to help prepare for Dr. Martin Luther King's Poor People's Campaign, and around the world with my new husband, Peter Edelman, including the war zones of Vietnam with John Paul Vann after Dr. King and Robert Kennedy were assassinated. This journey brought me to the founding of the Washington Research Project (WRP), a public interest law group, and the beginning of the Children's Defense Fund into which it evolved in 1973. I am grateful beyond words for the example of the lanterns shared in this memoir whose lives I hope will illuminate my children's, your children's, and the paths of countless others coming behind.

In many ways, the labyrinth of my life is leading back to where I began and to many of the lessons learned but too easily lost in the cacophony of noise and clutter and triviality and depersonalization afflicting so much of modern American life and culture. With others, I seek to reweave the frayed remnants of family, community, and spiritual values rent asunder in the name of progress. That much racial, social, and scientific progress has taken place over my lifetime is evident. Millions of Black children and poor children of all races have moved into the American mainstream and are better off materially. But something important has been lost as we have thrown away or traded so much of our Black spiritual heritage for a false sense of economic security and inclusion. We are at risk of letting our children drown in the bathwater of American materialism, greed, and violence. We must regain our moral bearings and roots and help America recover hers before millions more children—Black, Brown, and White, poor, middle-class, and rich—self-destruct or grow up thinking life is about acquiring rather than sharing, selfishness rather than sacrifice, and material rather than spiritual wealth.

I do not seek to go back to the segregated indignities of the days before *Brown v. Board of Education* [the 1954 Supreme Court ruling that desegregated public schools] and am grateful beyond words for the Civil Rights Movement which I was blessed to witness, share in, and benefit from, as did all Americans. So few human beings have been blessed, as I have been, to experience firsthand the convergence of such great events and great leaders. The sacrifices of Montgomery, Birmingham, and Selma, Alabama, of Jackson, Mississippi and Memphis, Tennessee to tear down America's iron curtain of racial segregation must never be forgotten or repeated. We must fight with all our might the racial, religious, and gender intolerance and hate crimes resurging today in our schools, homes, and communities. Black citizens gained the right we should always have had to sit anywhere on a bus and in a restaurant, to drink colorless water without the indignity of separate Black and White fountains, to play in public playgrounds and read in public libraries, and to escape decrepit schools without books, supplies, and well-paid teachers. But as Littleton, Colorado's massacre of children by children, New York City's police brutality, and a recent Texas lynching demonstrate, skin color or "differences" defined by someone's arbitrary standards can still trigger unjust violence.

Successes and Remaining Challenges

The Civil Rights Movement immeasurably lightened the physical, mental, and emotional burden of growing up Black in America. My children and yours may find it unimaginable that my generation was not able to go to the bathroom when we had to, to drink when we were thirsty, and to eat when we were hungry—natural behaviors that required unnatural thought and preparation if you were a Black child growing up in the segregated South. What Black adult today does not painfully recall holding in urine as our parents searched for a place to stop? Who in my generation was not accustomed to packing lunches to eat in the car because there was no restaurant where we could stop and be served? And who among us cannot regurgitate the feelings of rage and resentment from having to "stay in your place" watch your words, cover your back, and hide your fear, the consequences of being born Black or different from prevailing cultural standards of beauty or acceptability.

Yet as I drive past the endless clutter of fast food restaurants on our interstates and ugly sprawling city outskirts, and am glad to be able to stop and eat and go to the bathroom, I wonder whether all the hamburgers and fries and fried chicken, which I so love, are good for me, my children, or anybody's health. I worry about the loss of dinner rituals—preparing balanced meals together, setting the table, family conversation—in this era of fast foods and instant gratification. I worry about how children will learn to cook and develop good table manners and conversational skills without seeing and doing these things regularly with parents and other adults. I worry about children not feeling useful and not learning how to take care of themselves and of their families and others through regular chores. And I worry about millions of children not learning in public schools how to read and write and compute at grade level and failing behind in our knowledge-based national and global economies. Providing *all* our children—ninety percent of whom are in public schools, the crucible of our democracy—equitable and quality education is a challenge the world's super power is failing to meet today at its peril. Military readiness is hollow if our children are not school-ready. National security means nothing if a child is not safe at home and at school.

Finally, I look around with concern at the loneliness and neediness of so many children who are trying so hard to grow up and who need parents, and other caring, reliable adults to see, hear, listen to, and spend time with them in our too careless, too fast, too busy culture. So many children are killing themselves and others because they lack enough adults in their homes, schools, communities, public life, and culture to show them a different way and to reflect lives with positive purpose and integrity. Adult hypocrisy is confusing and deadening our children's spirits and minds as they struggle through an American landmine of drugs, guns, violence, and greed poised to shatter their bodies, minds, dreams, and futures.

The Unfinished Quest for Justice
But I look ahead with faith and determination, firmly believing we can together build newer healthier lives,

strong families, strong communities, and strong children who are good human beings. This will require reshaping national priorities and reclaiming the enduring values of compassion, fairness, and opportunity that are the bedrock of the great experiment called America.

I celebrated my sixtieth birthday in 1999 (I can't believe it and don't feel it!) and am blessed with a good husband, three great adult sons, enough money, and more honors than I can pack away. And yet I feel an urgent need to throw all caution to the winds and to risk all to try to finish the quest for justice and inclusion that our founding fathers dreamed of but did not have the courage to constitutionalize and practice. Abraham Lincoln, Harriet Tubman, Sojourner Truth, Frederick Douglass, Elizabeth Cady Stanton, Eleanor Roosevelt, Benjamin Elijah Mays, Martin Luther King, Jr., Dorothy Day, Fannie Lou Hamer, Rosa Parks, Septima Clark, Ella Baker, Charles Houston, and Thurgood Marshall did their part to finish America's unfinished symphony of freedom and justice. It is now time for the next great movement, for our children. It must be led by mothers and grandmothers of all races and faiths, with youths and all others who want to show the world that America is decent enough and sensible enough and moral enough to take care of all of its children. I invite you to join me in the urgent crusade to Leave No Child Behind® so that one hundred and one thousand years from now, our children's children will call us blessed and God will say "well done," as I know God has said or will say to the lanterns I thank in this book.

Maxine Waters

Chris Warren

Challenging the common misconception that overt racial
unrest is mostly confined to the American South is Los
Angeles, the nation's second-largest city. Two of late
twentieth-century America's most notorious civil uprisings
occurred in Los Angeles: the Watts riots of 1965 and the
1992 riots after a jury acquitted four white policemen
charged with the videotaped beating of black motorist
Rodney King. Yet despite its reputation for gang violence,
drug crimes, and racial tensions, South-Central Los Angeles is also a vibrant multicultural community where the majority of citizens are committed to protecting their families
and neighborhoods from the urban woes that plague most
American cities. One of their fiercest advocates is their representative to the U.S. Congress, Maxine Waters (1938–).
A member of the Black Congressional Caucus and an outspoken liberal Democrat, Waters has butted heads with
members of her own political party when she has felt that
its policies neglected the concerns of her constituents. The
following profile by Chris Warren of *Los Angeles* magazine
examines Waters's career and how her early life, as one of
thirteen children in a poor St. Louis family, influenced her
strong sense of political purpose. Published in 1998, Warren's profile also recounts Waters's ardent opposition to
President Bill Clinton's impeachment, a position she steadfastly maintained throughout the national ordeal.

❦ ❦ ❦

Maxine Waters has just one foot out of her black Town Car before a stranger recognizes her. "Hey, Ms. Waters," the man yells from across bustling Central Avenue in South Los Angeles. The congresswoman's car has rolled to a halt in front of a large clay-colored job-training facility, a project she helped bring to fruition here in the '80s while still a member of the California legislature. The man gives her a thumbs-up, and Waters returns the greeting with a bright smile and an enthusiastic wave.

Although this complex—the Maxine Waters Employment Preparation Center—is not in her current congressional district, Waters is clearly not forgotten here. As she strolls down the sun-baked sidewalk explaining the services the center offers—a computer lab, employment preparation for welfare mothers—Waters is continually interrupted by honking cars and well-wishers.

In a city where relatively few people even vote, let alone know who their elected representatives are, Maxine Waters is practically a celebrity. Her high profile is a result of the congresswoman's insistence that she be seen and heard. An outspoken, hard-line liberal Democrat, Waters, 60, has a history of grabbing headlines, twisting arms and intimidating opponents to ensure that her mostly minority, lower-income constituents not only get their fair share of federal money and programs, but are represented at the highest levels of government.

Translating Outrage into Action
"She's a pit bull. She doesn't beat around the bush, and that's a style, I think, that's effective," says Mayor Richard Riordan, who calls on Waters regularly for ad-

vice. "I don't know anybody I'd rather have on my side in a political fight than Maxine Waters." Adds U.S. Senator Barbara Boxer: "I think she sees injustice and gets outraged. She puts that outrage into action, and she's consistently speaking for those who don't have a voice."

After four terms in Congress and 22 years in elected office, Waters has such an electoral stranglehold on her South L.A. district that her reelection is a foregone conclusion. But she is approaching this November's [1998] race with the kind of urgency and energy usually displayed by a challenger closing in on a vulnerable incumbent. Waters is furiously raising money and traveling around the country to support other Democratic candidates, because she believes that taking the House back from Newt Gingrich and the Republicans is absolutely vital to advancing issues she cares about, issues like affirmative action and funds for inner-city economic development.

"People like me who are considered too liberal and too progressive are not usually listened to. We are considered, at this point in time, to be out of the mainstream of what government should deliver and what politics should be about," she says. "We don't get to take up our issues. Our members get voted down unless it's an unusual situation. And it doesn't feel good to lose day in and day out."

Waters wants her voice to really matter again. Republicans casually dismiss her as a political anachronism: an old-school liberal wedded to the discredited idea that big government can solve all of society's problems. Predictably, the opposition chafes at her aggressive, in-your-face style. But some local African-American politicians also intensely dislike what they say is her loud, bullying, spotlight-grabbing way of doing things. They consider Waters divisive and counter-productive and question just how effective she has been at finding solutions to problems and getting results for her constituents.

None of the criticism, though, has kept Waters from becoming one of the most high-profile, influential African-American politicians in the country. In 1996, after just six years in Congress, she was elected to both the House Democratic leadership as well as the chair of the powerful Congressional Black Caucus. Waters also has strong ties to the [Bill] Clinton administration. She served as national cochair for Clinton's 1992 campaign, was instrumental in persuading the President to visit Africa last spring, and her husband, Sidney Williams, was appointed by Clinton as ambassador to the Bahamas.

Despite all this, she has bitterly opposed the administration at times. In 1994, she was arrested outside the White House for protesting Clinton's Haitian refugee policy, and last year she condemned the President's welfare reform initiative as too harsh and inflexible. "I'd just as soon battle Clinton as battle someone I see doing something wrong on the street," she says.

Waters's Hands-On Representation

But Beltway politics and maneuvering seem far away on this balmy afternoon in L.A. As Waters walks back to her car, she stopped by a young woman who is near tears. (She had crossed the street from the County Department of Public Social Services when she saw the congresswoman drive up.) Waters listens to her intently, then accompanies her back across the street and into the office. The woman, penniless and with no place to stay that night, had been turned away, told she was in the wrong office to apply for shelter and needed to go to Norwalk, more than 10 miles away, to fill out the proper paperwork.

"We're going to try to get her some help," Waters says as she disappears behind a supervisor's door. Fifteen minutes later, she and the young woman, now smiling, reappear. A few words from Waters are enough to cut through the red tape and get her a place to stay for the next two weeks.

Waters's aides say she is constantly doing this kind of hands-on constituent work, trying to solve people's problems on the spot. "It is a real understanding I have about the unfairness of the inability of poor and powerless people to get a decent shake from the government and from life in general," she explains. It is a deep sense of empathy, friends say, born of her own life experiences. "Maxine learned some early lessons about fighting for what you believe in, saying what you mean and meaning what you say," says Kweisi Mfume, national president of the NAACP and a former chair of the Black Caucus. "She developed, in my opinion, a very clear understanding of what is to be poor, dispossessed and without a lot of power."

Childhood Experiences

The story of Waters's life seems never far from her mind, even in the midst of a hectic day traveling around her district during the congressional summer recess. After announcing a $709,000 NASA grant she obtained to help students at South-Central's George Washington Preparatory High School improve their math, science and language skills, Waters addresses the crowd of mostly black and Latino kids packed into the school library. "I was born in St. Louis, Missouri. I have 12 brothers and sisters. We were on welfare most of my life. Off and on welfare. So we were very, very poor," she tells the attentive audience.

"But guess what? Many of us learned at some point in our lives to just take responsibility for ourselves no matter what's going on," she continues, her voice quickening and gaining force. "If you put a little more effort into it, no matter what's going on at home, you can do it. We believe that. And that's why we're here."

It's a speech Waters will make more than once on this day and one that crystallizes her philosophy that the role of government is to help people—particularly the poor—improve the quality of their lives. It's a philosophy Waters formed long before she was elected to the California legislature in 1976, her first political office.

Waters started working when she was 12, clearing tables in a segregated restaurant where black employees had to eat their meals in the basement. Like her mother, Waters married young and began having children. Unlike her mother, she continued to pursue her education, balancing her time working, raising kids and intermittently going to college. She moved to Los Angeles in 1960 and eventually landed a job as an assistant teacher with Head Start, the federal program aimed at preparing underprivileged preschool children for elementary school. "In many ways, Head Start changed my life. I was inspired to stay in college," says Waters, who graduated from Cal State L.A. in 1971 with a B.A. in sociology. "But the most important thing about the program was that it helped you to understand that you had talent, you had ideas, you had thoughts and you could do things," she says.

Early Political Involvement

Waters was introduced to politics while at Head Start, when she became involved in lobbying elected officials for program funding. She started volunteering on the campaigns of politicians friendly toward the program, gradually becoming interested in politics as a career. "I had always wanted to be a social worker because the social worker was the authority figure I saw in my life during those days on welfare," she says. "And I thought that if I could only be a social worker, then I could really help people." But she soon found that it was the politicians who had the most potential to make a difference.

Waters threw herself into politics, working on the campaigns of black candidates like state senator Mervyn Dymally and Mayor Tom Bradley. In 1976, when the California assembly member from her district decided to leave office, Waters was urged to run, particularly by other women. Because of her extensive campaign experience, she had no problem organizing her own, and this background made connecting with people and seeking votes even easier. "There's something I like about being out on the street with people," she says. "It feels right for me."

In her 14 years in the California legislature, Waters was a major power player. She helped Willie Brown become speaker of the assembly in 1980 and was able to exert tremendous influence as a result of their close relationship. She was the driving force behind legislation divesting state money from firms that did business with South Africa's apartheid regime. And she continued to champion the dispossessed, fighting for job-training programs, affordable housing and the end of police strip searches of nonviolent offenders.

Confrontation and Criticism

Since being elected to Congress in 1990, Waters has gained a reputation among her critics for being confrontational and for making the issue of race the determining factor in many of her decisions and initiatives. There is also the question of how effective she is in getting legislation passed. "People aren't sure how many votes she can bring to a particular issue," says a former Democratic staffer on Capitol Hill. "And the hotter her rhetoric, the fewer people she brings with her."

To illustrate how divisive her tactics can be, opponents point to an incident on the House floor in the summer of 1994. New York congressman Peter King, a

Republican who serves with Waters on the Banking Committee, was cross-examining Hillary Clinton's chief of staff, Margaret Williams, an African American, about Whitewater. Waters did not like King's line of questioning and yelled at him to "shut up," causing a shouting match between the two that was broadcast on ABC's *Nightline* that evening as an example of the deterioration of manners in Congress.

King says House GOP members expect this kind of behavior from Waters: "The objection that most Republicans have—and I'm sure she couldn't care what our objections are—is that she is very partisan, very quick to raise the race card and almost always trying to inflame the issue rather than find any common ground." Adds Larry Elder, a black radio talk show host for KABC in L.A.: "Maxine Waters, in my opinion, embodies the worst of the elements that pass for black leadership today. [Her] message is, The route [to success] is not hard work. The route is not doing your homework. The route is not forgoing dribbling a basketball or hanging out with your homeys. The route is to have government somehow, someway come riding to the rescue on a white horse."

Waters sits in her office at the end of a day that has taken her from one corner of her district to another. By now, she is used to the criticism and takes it all with a level of equanimity. She understands that the image many have of her is diametrically opposed to the one she has of herself. Indeed, watching her interact with her staff and constituents, one has the sense that she takes almost a parental interest in everyone she meets. She looks people in the eye, sometimes holds their hand long after she's finished shaking it and gives them her undivided attention. It doesn't matter whether it's a corporate executive or an ex-gang member in a training program.

"I think that my strong position and my advocacy are what my constituents really want and like," says Waters. "I make things happen, and I have credibility with the people I care about."

She points to the work she has done on the federal level—including procuring $10 trillion in loan guarantees to cities for economic development in 1992 and a $50 million appropriation for a Youth Fair Chance program to help prepare unskilled, unemployed young adults for the workforce—as examples of how she's helped better the lives of her constituents. She is currently working on developing a portion of L.A's Vermont Avenue, with help from Nike.

Her Position on Impeachment

Waters's term as chair of the Black Caucus is ending, and she is looking forward to pursuing some "profound" long-term goals, like redefining the mission of the intelligence community and "getting a handle on the influx of drugs into this country." She seems extraordinarily energetic and eager to continue fighting for her principles. One fight she may soon find herself embroiled in will be the battle over the future of Bill Clinton's presidency. As a member of the House Judiciary Committee, she will be one of 36 representatives who will determine whether independent counsel Kenneth Starr has amassed enough evidence against the President to warrant full-blown impeachment hearings.

Although Waters was at first mum on l'affaire Clinton, as soon as Starr released his official report in September, she appeared on NBC's *Meet the Press* and CNN's *Crossfire*, vowing that the Black Caucus would act as the "fairness police" in any impeachment proceeding. Yet she still sounds partisan when she speaks about the House Republicans.

"As soon as I have the opportunity, I am going to talk

about the Hillary Clinton that conservatives wish their wives could be in times of adversity," she declares. "Hold that family together, no matter what. Stick with your husband, no matter what. But they are not going to give her credit for that."

Waters is prepared to defend Clinton and even seems to accept the First Lady's theory of a vast conspiracy to bring the administration down. "I think the right wing feels absolutely threatened by Hillary and Bill Clinton," she says. "Through their good work, they have caused the right wing to turn on progressive politics in ways that people never thought could happen again in this country. It has been clever, it has been orchestrated, and they have been effective in what they've been able to do."

Though Waters doesn't shy away from such battles, the brutal, very personal way politics is practiced today gives her pause. "The most unfortunate thing about politics is this increasing notion that the way to win is to dirty you up and put you in jail," she says.

And Waters, who admits she can be contentious and aggressive, thinks that the politics of personal destruction are unnecessary. There is a way, she says, to disagree with an opponent without going for the throat. "I have the ability to listen, even if I am going to disagree. And I disagree a lot. But I can do it in a way that does not necessarily disrespect them," she says. "But they have also learned that I cannot be run over. I cannot be abused. I cannot be disrespected."

Appendix of Documents

Document 1: The Political Future of American Women

A poet, novelist, and educator as well as dedicated abolitionist and women's rights activist, Frances Ellis Watkins Harper (1825–1911) was among the most accomplished women of nineteenth-century America. In an 1893 address excerpted below, Harper advocates women's full political participation in the postslavery United States.

If before sin had cast its deepest shadows or sorrow had distilled its bitterest tears, it was true that it was not good for man to be alone, it is no less true, since the shadows have deepened and life's sorrows have increased, that the world has need of all the spiritual aid that woman can give for the social advancement and moral development of the human race. The tendency of the present age, with its restlessness, religious upheavals, failures, blunders, and crimes, is toward broader freedom, an increase of knowledge, the emancipation of thought, and a recognition of the brotherhood of man; in this movement woman as the companion of man, must be a sharer. So close is the bond between man and woman that you can not raise one without lifting the other. The world can not move without woman's sharing in the movement, and to help give a right impetus to that movement is woman's highest privilege. . . .

As the saffron tints and crimson flushes of morn herald the coming day, so the social and political advancement which woman has already gained bears the promise of the rising of the full-orbed sun of emancipation. The result will not be to make the home less happy, but society more holy; yet I do not think the mere extension of the ballot a panacea for all the ills of our national life. What we need today is not simply more voters, but better voters. Today there are red-handed men in our republic, who walk unwhipped of justice, who richly deserve to exchange the ballot of the freeman for the wristlets of the felon; brutal and cowardly men, who torture, burn, and lynch their fellow men, men whose defenselessness should be their best defense and their weakness an ensign of protection. More than the changing of institutions we need the development of a national conscience, and the upbuilding of national character. Men may boast of the aristocracy of blood, may glory in the aristocracy of talent, and be proud of the aristocracy of wealth, but there is one aristocracy which must ever outrank them all, and that is the aristocracy of character, and it is the women of a country who help to mold its character; and to influence if not determine its destiny; and in the political future of our nation woman will not have done what she could if she does not endeavor to have our republic stand foremost among the nations of the earth, wearing sobriety as a crown and righteousness a garment and a girdle. In coming into her political estate woman will find a mass of illiteracy to be dispelled. If knowledge is power, ignorance is also power. The power that educates wickedness may manipulate and dash against the pillars of any state when they are undermined and honeycombed by injustice.

"Woman's Political Future—Address by Frances E.W. Harper of Virginia," 1893, in May Wright Sewall, ed., *The World's Congress of Representative Women*. Chicago: Rand McNally, 1894, pp. 433–37.

Document 2: "Woman Suffrage Has Never Kept Me Awake at Night"

Margaret Murray Washington (1863–1953), wife of Booker T. Washington, was an educator as well as active in the National Association for Colored Women. Her views about social change were conservative, as evidenced in her ambivalence about woman suffrage in the following commentary from 1895.

Suffrage.—Colored women, quite as much as colored men, realize that if there is ever to be equal justice and fair play in the protection in the courts everywhere for all races, then there must be an equal chance for all women as well as men to express their preference through their votes. There are certain things so sure to come our way that time in arguing them is not well spent. It is simply the cause of right which in the end always conquers, no matter how fierce the opposition. Personally woman suffrage has never kept me awake at night, but I am sure before this country is able to take its place amongst the great democratic nations of the earth it has got to come to the place where it is willing to trust its citizens, black as well as white, women as well as men, to be loyal to their Government, to be willing to leave the carrying out of governmental offices to the intelligent part of the citizenship. Our Department of Suffrage conducts training classes in the constitution of the country, and has given time to the study of all governmental affairs, so that women may be prepared to handle the vote intelligently and wisely when it comes to them. Thousands of our women vote in the Northern States where they live, and in no instance have they shown any disposition to assume control of affairs, nor have they presumed anything more than a desire to be counted as a citizen of a country where they are giving the best of themselves in building better homes, better schools, better churches, and finally better citizenship.

Margaret Murray Washington, "Club Work Among Negro Women," 1895, in J.L. Nichols and William Crogman, eds., *Progress of a Race*. Rev. ed. Naperville, Illinois: J.L. Nichols, 1929, pp. 178, 182, 192–95, 209. Reprinted in Gerda Lerner, ed., *Black Women in White America: A Documentary History*. New York: Vintage Books, 1972, p. 446.

Document 3: The Importance of Black Women's Organizations

Born into one of Boston's elite families, Josephine St. Pierre Ruffin (1842–1924) was an activist, philanthropist, and journalist who edited and published The Woman's Era, *the first newspaper published by and for black American women. The following ex-*

*cerpt, from an address that appeared in an 1895 issue of the pa-
per, argues that black women's organizations and clubs help to
counter the prevailing racist stereotypes about women of color.*

All over the America there is to be found a large and growing class of earnest, intelligent, progressive colored women,
women who, if not leading full useful lives, are only waiting
for the opportunity to do so, many of them warped and
cramped for lack of opportunity, not only to do more but to
be more; and yet, if an estimate of the colored women of
America is called for, the inevitable reply, glibly given, is,
"For the most part ignorant and immoral, some exceptions,
of course, but these don't count."

Now for the sake of the thousands of self-sacrificing young
women teaching and preaching in lonely southern back-
woods[,] for the noble army of mothers who have given birth
to these girls, mothers whose intelligence is only limited by
their opportunity to get books, for the sake of the fine cul-
tured women who have carried off the honors in school here
and often abroad, for the sake of our own dignity, the dignity
of our race, and the future good name of our children, it is
"mete, right and our bounden duty" to stand forth and de-
clare ourselves and principles, to teach an ignorant and sus-
picious world that our aims and interests are identical with
those of all good aspiring women. Too long have we been
silent under unjust and unholy charges; we cannot expect to
have them removed until we disprove them through ourselves. It is not enough to try to disprove unjust charges
through individual effort, that never goes any further. Year
after year southern women have protested against the admis-
sion of colored women into any national organization on the
ground of the immorality of these women, and because all
refutation has only been tried by individual work the charge
has never been crushed, as it could and should have been at
the first. Now with an army of organized women standing for
purity and mental worth, we in ourselves deny the charges
and open the eyes of the world to a state of affairs to which
they have been blind, often willfully so, and the very fact that
the charges, audaciously and flippantly made, as they often

are, are of so humiliating and delicate a nature, serves to protect the accuser by driving the helpless accused into mortified
silence. It is to break this silence, not by noisy protestations
of what we are not, but by a dignified showing of what we are
and hope to become that we are impelled to take this step, to
make of this gathering an object lesson to the world. For
many and apparent reasons it is especially fitting that the
women of the race take the lead in this movement, but for all
this we recognize the necessity of the sympathy of our husbands, brothers and fathers.

Our woman's movement is woman's in that it is led and directed by women for the good of women and men, for the
benefit of all humanity, which is more than any one branch
or section of it. We want, we ask the active interest of our
men, and, too, we are not drawing the color line; we are
women, American women, as intensely interested in all that
pertains to us as such as all other American women; we are
not alienating or withdrawing, we are only coming to the
front, willing to join any others in the same work and cor-
dially inviting and welcoming any others to join us.

"Address of Josephine St. P. Ruffin," *The Woman's Era*, vol. 2, no. 5, August 1895.

Document 4: The Power and Potential of Black Women

*In the following excerpt from her 1897 inaugural address to the
National Association of Colored Women, president Mary Church
Terrell invokes the group's governing principles, primary goals,
and black women's potential for greatness.*

Acting upon this principle of concentration and union have
the colored women of the United States banded themselves
together to fulfill a mission to which they feel peculiarly
adapted and especially called. We have become *National*, because from the Atlantic to the Pacific, from Maine to the
Gulf, we wish to set in motion influences that shall stop the
ravages made by practices that sap our strength and preclude
the possibility of advancement, which under other circum-

stances could easily be made. We call ourselves an *Association* to signify that we have joined hands one with the other to work together in a common cause. We proclaim to the world that the women of our race have become partners in the great firm of progress and reform. We denominate ourselves colored, not because we are narrow, and wish to lay special emphasis on the color of the skin, for which no one is responsible, which of itself is no proof neither of an individual's virtue nor of his vice, which is a stamp neither of one's intelligence nor of ignorance, but we refer to the fact that this is an association of colored women, because our peculiar status in this country at the present time seems to demand that we stand by ourselves in the special work for which we have organized. For this reason it was thought best to invite the attention of the world to the fact that colored women feel their responsibility as a unit, and together have clasped hands to assume it.

Special stress is laid upon the fact that our association is composed of women, not because we wish to deny rights and privileges to our brothers in imitation of the example they have set for us so many years, but because the work which we hope to accomplish can be done better, we believe, by the mothers, wives, daughters, and sisters of our race than by the fathers, husbands, brothers, and sons. The crying need of our organization of colored women is questioned by no one conversant with our peculiar trials and perplexities, and acquainted with the almost insurmountable obstacles in our path to those attainments and acquisitions to which it is the right and privilege of every member of every race to aspire.

It is not because we are discouraged at the progress made by our people that we have uttered the cry of alarm which has called together this band of earnest women assembled here tonight. In the unprecedented advancement made by the Negro since his emancipation, we take great pride and extract therefore both courage and hope. From a condition of dense ignorance but thirty years ago, we have advanced so far in the realm of knowledge and letters as to have produced scholars and authors of no mean repute. Though penniless as a race a short while ago, we have among us today a few men of wealth and multitudes who own their homes and make comfortable livings. We therefore challenge any other race to present a record more creditable and show a progress more wonderful than that made by the ex-slaves of the United States of America and that too in the face of prejudice, proscription, and persecution against which no other people has ever had to contend in the history of the world. And yet while rejoicing in our steady march onward and upward to the best and highest things of life, we are nevertheless painfully mindful of our weakness and defects. While we know the Negro is no worse than other races equally poor, equally ignorant, and equally oppressed, we would nevertheless see him lay aside the sins that do so easily beset him, and come forth clothed in all these attributes of mind and grace of character that claims the real man. To accomplish this end through the simple, swiftest, surest methods, the colored women have organized themselves into this Association, whose power for good, let us hope, will be as enduring as it is unlimited.

Mary Church Terrell, "First Presidential Address to the National Association of Colored Women," Nashville, Tennessee, September 15, 1897. Mary Church Terrell Papers, Library of Congress (Microfilm, reel 20, frames 511–22).

Document 5: A Call for Unity Among Black and White Women

Adella Hunt Logan (1863–1915) was the first librarian at the Tuskegee Institute, where she also taught English and social sciences. She was also an activist who lectured on the topic of women's right to vote, a cause she ardently supported. In the following selection, she argues for a closer working relationship between the National Association of Colored Women and National Council of Women and other white feminist organizations.

The preamble of the constitution of the National Council of Women of the United States, contains these words: "We women of the United States, sincerely believing that the best good of our homes and nation will be advanced by our own greater unity of thought, sympathy and purpose, and that an organized movement of women will best conserve the highest good of the family and the State, do hereby unite ourselves in a confederation of workers, committed to the overthrow of all forms of ignorance and injustice, and to the application of the golden rule to society, custom and law."

Some people facetiously, others derisively, say that the Negro is of no nation. So far is this from being true, that the so-classed Negro people are of many nations. Any people thus mixed would demand great thought for its life, but when such a mixed race, with its various grades of civilization, are classed and treated according to the lowest grades within its ranks, then the problems of its life become peculiarly complex and difficult.

Many of the best women of this race are club women. If Anglo-American women feel their need of greater unity of thought, sympathy and purpose, and resort to organized effort to overthrow ignorance and injustice, how much more do Afro-Americans need to see and feel the advantages of greater unity of thought, sympathy and purpose? And how infinitely more do the latter need to band together and overthrow ignorance and injustice, and to bring about the application of the golden rule to society.

Why join the National Council of Women? Because we are American women and the council exists to promote the welfare of all women of the country. We do not, of course, expect or desire direct help from any organization without contributing our quota to the life of said organization. . . .

Ignorance of each other is at the bottom of the prejudice existing between the races. This ignorance is the natural and direct outcome of separation. There are valuable lessons to be learned both races by a closer relationship.

Adella Hunt Logan, "Why the National Association of Colored Women Should Become Part of the National Council of Women of the United States," *The National Association Notes*, vol. 3, no. 8, December 1899, p. 1 (NACW microfilm, part 1, reel 23, frames 326–27).

Document 6: The Black Panther National Anthem

Radical activist and author Elaine Brown (1943–) was one of the leading female members of the Black Panther Party, elected as the party head in 1974. In 1969 the Black Panther *newspaper published the organization's national anthem, composed by Brown and invoking the spirit and inspiration of slain black leader Malcolm X.*

Black Panther National Anthem

Yes—He turned and he walked
Past the eyes of my life.
And, he nodded and sang without sound.
And his face had the look
Of a man who knew strife
And a feeling familiarly came around.

REFRAIN

    I said,
    Man, where have you been for all these years
    Man, where were you when I sought you
    Man, do you know me as I know you
    Man, am I coming through

And, he spoke in a voice
That was centuries old.
And, he smiled in a way that was strange.
And, his full lips of night
Spoke about our people's plight
And a feeling familiarly came around.

REFRAIN

And, we sat and we talked
About freedom and things.
And, he told me about what he dreamed.
But I knew of that dream
Long before he had spoke
And a feeling familiarly came around.

REFRAIN

Elaine Brown, "Black Panther National Anthem," published in the *Black Panther* newspaper, April 27, 1969.

Document 7: A Plea for Equality

Shirley Chisholm (1924–) was the first African American woman elected to the U.S. Congress. A dedicated feminist as well as civil rights activist, Chisholm was an early supporter of the Equal Rights Amendment. In the following speech before Congress, Chisholm makes an impassioned plea for sexual and racial equality.

Mr. Speaker, when a young woman graduates from college and starts looking for a job, she is likely to have a frustrating and even demeaning experience ahead of her. If she walks into an office for an interview, the first question she will be asked is, "Do you type?"

There is a calculated system of prejudice that lies unspoken behind that question. Why is it acceptable for women to be secretaries, librarians, and teachers, but totally unacceptable for them to be managers, administrators, doctors, lawyers, and Members of Congress.

The unspoken assumption is that women are different. They do not have executive ability, orderly minds, stability, leadership skills, and they are too emotional.

It has been observed before, that society for a long time, discriminated against another minority, the blacks, on the same basis—that they were different and inferior. The happy little homemaker and the contented "old darkey" on the plantation were both produced by prejudice.

As a black person, I am no stranger to race prejudice. But the truth is that in the political world I have been far oftener discriminated against because I am a woman than because I am black.

Prejudice against blacks is becoming unacceptable although it will take years to eliminate it. But it is doomed because, slowly, white America is beginning to admit that it exists. Prejudice against women is still acceptable. There is very little understanding yet of the immorality involved in double pay scales and the classification of most of the better jobs as "for men only."

More than half of the population of the United States is female. But women occupy only 2 percent of the managerial positions. They have not even reached the level of tokenism yet. No women sit on the AFL-CIO council or Supreme Court. There have been only two women who have held Cabinet rank, and at present there are none. Only two women now hold ambassadorial rank in the diplomatic corps. In Congress, we are down to one Senator and 10 Representatives.

Considering that there are about 3½ million more women in the United States than men, this situation is outrageous. . . .

It is for this reason that I wish to introduce today a proposal that has been before every Congress for the last 40 years and that sooner or later must become part of the basic law of the land—the equal rights amendment. . . .

It is obvious that discrimination exists. Women do not have the opportunities that men do. And women that do not conform to the system, who try to break with the accepted patterns, are stigmatized as "odd" and "unfeminine." The fact is that a woman who aspires to be chairman of the board, or a Member of the House, does so for exactly the same reasons as any man. Basically, these are that she thinks she can do the job and she wants to try.

Shirley Chisholm, address to the U.S. House of Representatives, Washington, DC, May 21, 1969.

Document 8: Why Nixon Must Be Impeached

Barbara Jordan (1936–1996) was the first black woman elected to the Texas state senate, and in 1972, became the first black woman from the South to serve in the U.S. Congress. A leading member of the House Judiciary Committee convened to weigh the possible impeachment of President Richard M. Nixon, Congresswoman Jordan spoke forcefully about the sanctity of the Constitution and the gravity of Nixon's offenses. The following is an excerpt from her opening statement to the committee.

Earlier today we heard the beginning of the Preamble to the Constitution of the United States, *We, the people.* It is a very eloquent beginning. But when that document was completed, on the seventeenth of September in 1787, I was not included in that *We, the people.* I felt somehow for many years that George Washington and Alexander Hamilton just left me out by mistake. But through the process of amendment, interpretation, and court decision I have finally been included in *We, the people.*

Today I am an inquisitor. I believe hyperbole would not be fictional and would not overstate the solemness that I feel right now. My faith in the Constitution is whole, it is complete, it is total. I am not going to sit here and be an idle spectator to the diminution, the subversion, the destruction of the Constitution. . . .

Beginning shortly after the Watergate break-in and continuing to the present time, the president has engaged in a series of public statements and actions designed to thwart the lawful investigation by government prosecutors. Moreover, the president has made public announcements and assertions bearing on the Watergate case which the evidence will show he knew to be false.

These assertions, false assertions, impeachable, those who misbehave. Those who "behave amiss or betray their public trust."

James Madison again at the Constitutional Convention: "A president is impeachable if he attempts to subvert the Constitution."

The Constitution charges the president with the task of taking care that the laws be faithfully executed, and yet the president has counseled his aides to commit perjury, willfully disregarded the secrecy of grand jury proceedings, concealed surreptitious entry, attempted to compromise a federal judge while publicly displaying his cooperation with the processes of criminal justice.

"A president is impeachable if he attempts to subvert the Constitution."

If the impeachment provision in the Constitution of the United States will not reach the offenses charged here, then perhaps that eighteenth century Constitution should be abandoned to a twentieth-century paper shredder. Has the president committed offenses and planned and directed and acquiesced in a course of conduct which the Constitution will not tolerate? That is the question. We know that. We know the question. We should now forthwith proceed to answer the question. It is reason, and not passion, which must guide our deliberations, guide our debate, and guide our decision.

Barbara Jordan, opening statement to the House Judiciary Committee Proceedings on Impeachment of Richard Nixon. Washington, DC, July 25, 1974.

Document 9: A Black Feminist Manifesto

The Combahee River Collective (CRC) was founded in 1974 by a small group of radical black feminists, including Barbara Smith and Demeta Frazier out of the Boston chapter of the National Black Feminist Organization (NBFO). The group's 1977 statement, excerpted below, articulates the CRC's explicit commitment to revolutionary political change and its solidarity with Socialist and gay rights movements in addition to mainstream feminist and civil rights ones.

We are a collective of Black feminists who have been meeting together since 1974 . . . involved in the process of defining and clarifying our politics, while . . . doing political work within our own group and in coalition with other progressive organizations and movements. . . . [W]e see Black feminism as the logical political movement to combat the manifold and simultaneous oppressions that all women of color face.

1. The Genesis of Contemporary Black Feminism

[W]e find our origins in the historical reality of Afro-American women's continuous life-and-death struggle for survival and liberation. . . . As Angela Davis points out, Black women have always embodied an adversary stance to white male rule and have actively resisted its inroads upon them and their communities. . . . Black, other Third World, and working women have been involved in the feminist movement from its start, but both outside reactionary forces and racism and elitism within the movement itself have served to obscure our participation. . . . Black feminist politics also have an obvious connection to movements for Black libera-

196   Black Women Activists

tion, particularly those of the 1960s and 1970s. . . . It was our experience and disillusionment within these liberation movements, as well as experience on the periphery of the white male left, that led to the need to develop a politics that was anti-racist, unlike those of white women, and anti-sexist, unlike those of Black and white men. There is also undeniably a personal genesis for Black feminism. . . . However, we had no way of conceptualizing what was so apparent to us, what we *knew* was really happening. . . . Our development must also be tied to the contemporary economic and political position of Black people. . . . [A] handful of us have been able to gain certain tools as a result of tokenism in education and employment which potentially enable us to more effectively fight our oppression. . . . [A]s we developed politically we addressed ourselves to heterosexism and economic oppression under capitalism.

2. What We Believe

Our politics evolve from a healthy love for ourselves, our sisters and our community which allows us to continue our struggle and work. This focusing upon our own oppression is embodied in the concept of identity politics. . . . [T]he most profound and potentially most radical politics come directly out of our own identity . . . [t]o be recognized as human, levelly human, is enough. . . . Although we are feminists and Lesbians, we feel solidarity with progressive Black men and do not advocate the fractionalization that white women who are separatists demand. . . . We struggle together with Black men against racism, while we also struggle with Black men about sexism. . . . We are socialists because we believe that work must be organized for the collective benefit of those who do the work and create the products, and not for the profit of the bosses. . . . We need to articulate the real class situation of persons . . . for whom racial and sexual oppression are significant determinants in their working/economic lives. . . . [O]ur Black women's style of talking/testifying in Black language about what we have experienced has a resonance that is both cultural and political. . . . No one before has ever examined the multilayered texture of Black women's lives. . . . "Smart-ugly" crystallized the way in which most of us had been forced to develop our intellects at great cost to our "social" lives. . . . We have a great deal of criticism and loathing for what men have been socialized to be in this society . . . [b]ut we do not have the misguided notion that it is their maleness, per se—i.e., their biological maleness—that makes them what they are.

3. Problems in Organizing Black Feminists

The major source of difficulty in our political work is that we are . . . trying . . . to address a whole range of oppressions. . . . We are dispossessed psychologically and on every other level, and yet we feel the necessity to struggle to change the condition of all Black women. . . . If Black women were free, it would mean that everyone else would have to be free since our freedom would necessitate the destruction of all the systems of oppression. Feminism is, nevertheless, very threatening to the majority of . . . people because it calls into question some of the most basic assumptions about our existence, i.e., that sex should be a determinant of power relationships. . . . We feel that it is absolutely essential to demonstrate the reality of our politics to other Black women and believe that we can do this through writing and distributing our work.

4. Black Feminist Issues and Projects

The inclusiveness of our politics makes us concerned with any situation that impinges upon the lives of women, Third World and working people. We are of course particularly committed to working on those struggles in which race, sex and class are simultaneously factors in oppression. . . . One issue that is of major concern to us and that we have begun to publicly address is racism in the white women's movement. . . . Eliminating racism in the white women's movement is by definition work for white women to do, but we will continue to speak to and demand accountability on this issue. . . . As feminists we do not want to mess over people in the name of politics. . . . We are committed to a continual examination of our politics as they develop through criticism and self-criticism as an essential aspect of our practice.

The Combahee River Collective Statement, 1986. www.buffalostate.edu/orgs/rspms/combahee.html.

Document 10: Black Americans' African Legacy

Civil rights attorney, law professor, feminist, poet, and ultimately, the first black American woman to be ordained an Episcopalian priest, Pauli Murray (1910–1985) led a life devoted to activism in service of social justice. In the following excerpt from her memoir Song in a Weary Throat, *Murray recounts her pilgrimage to Africa to witness firsthand the dignity and humanity of a people slandered by the white racist myth of "inferiority."*

I came to Africa, among other reasons, to see for myself black people in their own homeland and come to grips with the pervasive myth of innate racial inferiority that stigmatizes all people of discernible African descent in the United States. Although now widely discredited, this powerful myth shaped my growing years and gave me ambivalent feelings about myself. A remote African ancestry about which I knew little, linked with a heritage of slavery and continued inferior status in America, has been the source of a hidden shame. I need to confront the vestiges of shame embedded in my identity by making an on-the-spot assessment of my African background and my relationship to it. . . .

Traveling about the countryside, I have not only seen piercing reminders of a radical break with the African past but have also realized how subsequent distortions of this past to justify chattel slavery in the United States contributed to a legacy of shame. When I go to villages in the interior of Ghana, where the people continue to follow many of their ancient customs, I am struck by their innate dignity, their ceremonial courtesy, and their strong sense of community cooperation in building a house or road. Although they are nonliterate and have few belongings or creature comforts, they are rooted in their own land and have a strong sense of self. An African man may house his family in a mud hut, sleep on the ground, barely make a living scrabbling in parched earth, and have only one ceremonial cloth of cheap fabric. Yet when he drapes his toga about his shoulder and comes to greet a stranger, he walks with such self-assurance that I cannot help thinking how his proud bearing contrasts with the bearing of his sharecropper counterparts I have seen in rural America. I find myself pondering the great violence done to the human spirit through American slavery and its aftermath, originally in the name of "Christianizing black savages."

The contrast is even more sharply drawn when I visit a local chief seated on a raised platform in his inner courtyard, dressed in colorful robes and surrounded by his toga-clad council of village elders. An umbrella is held over his head and his linguist stands by to communicate his greetings and responses, although the chief understands and speaks fluent English. He receives visitors according to a formal ritual marked by gravity, which includes an exchange of gifts and the pouring of a libation from the visitor's gift of costly gin drop by drop upon the ground, accompanied by solemn incantations. Here again I saw the self-possession of black people whose spirits have not been crippled by generations of repression.

Pauli Murray, *Song in a Weary Throat: An American Pilgrimage*. New York: Harper & Row, 1987.

Document 11: The Power of Activism

In the following interview, Pulitzer Prize–winning novelist Alice Walker (1944–) discusses her social and political activism for causes ranging from halting female genital mutilation in Africa to ending U.S. sanctions against Cuba. Walker makes no apologies about using her talents as a writer in the service of human rights both at home and internationally.

If there's anything that has become clear about [Alice] Walker since her first book was published 29 years ago, it's that the Pulitzer Prize–winning author connects to people on her own terms. She is not bound by anyone's literary convention, custom or tradition. With regard to her commitment to addressing some of the most charged issues of the day, there's just no telling what Walker is likely to lay on us next.

For example, I would not be surprised if one day Alice Walker handed Supreme Court Justice Clarence Thomas a Sweet Honey in the Rock album, to help, in her words, "bring him back to the community."

"I wonder what Clarence would do if you just locked him in a room for five days with Bernice Johnson Reagon," says Walker, referring to the activist/leader of the acclaimed Washington, D.C–based singing group. "He is one of those people who has turned against his roots and Sweet Honey struggles constantly to affirm and uplift us. I bet Bernice could bring Clarence around."

While some of her critics (in the aftermath of the controversy surrounding *The Color Purple*) have accused her of having a "deep hatred of Blacks," Walker says it is love that prompts her to embrace individuals and issues others have shunned.

"I wrote about female genital mutilation hoping that one little girl born somewhere on the planet will not know its pain because of my work," Walker says about her efforts to end that practice. "And that in this one instance, at least, the pen will prove mightier than the circumciser's knife."

Mimi Ramsey, an Ethiopian woman who was herself mutilated as a child, underscores the impact of Walker's advocacy.

"She is my hero," Ramsey says with tears welling in her eyes. "Genital mutilation had been a taboo subject for 1,000 years before Alice Walker broke the ice. She made it financially possible for me to return to Ethiopia and confront my mother about her role in mutilating me. It was a very healing experience for us both."

It is with an equally fierce dedication to challenging "cruelty done in my name," that Walker decries the longstanding U.S. embargo against Cuba. In *Saved [Anything We Love Can Be Saved*, Walker's collection of essays on activism], readers will find several pieces detailing Walker's support of Fidel Castro, including a letter to President Clinton in which she lambastes a political policy that is, in her view, starving Cuban children.

"Would you want Chelsea to have no milk, to have one

egg a day?" Walker queries Clinton in her letter. "You are a large man, how would you yourself survive?" . . .

Anything We Love Can Be Saved is dedicated to, among others, Mumia Abu-Jamal, the Philadelphia Black Journalist currently on death row. University of Pittsburgh doctoral student, Cornell Womack, 30, helped to organize a reading that Walker, an ardent supporter of Mumia, gave to boost his legal defense.

"We passed the hat and because of Alice's participation, we raised more than $6,000," Womack says. "It was the single largest one-night contribution in the history of the Mumia movement."

But more important, Womack explains, is the activist model Walker offers for students searching to find real meaning during their college years.

"Alice has left an important legacy for young people in that she remains a simple, unpretentious woman who's interested in adding her wisdom and commitment to the movement, not in being a star." Womack says. "Her alchemy is such that everybody involved with the Mumia event felt that we'd made a friend. After it was over, Alice came to my house and we all ate and partied. She danced so hard that by the end of the evening she was soaked with sweat."

Walker says it's the good times that follow the hard times, as surely as day follows night, that keep her in the struggle for justice.

"Activism centers you, empowers you and basically makes you feel completely in the stream of life," she says joyfully. "For me, it's not drudgery, but rather about being bonded. Part of my message is that I enjoy activism and other people can, too. As an activist, you can have a really good time."

Evelyn C. White, "Activism on Campuses: Interview with Alice Walker," *The Black Collegian*, vol. 28, October 1997, p. 136. Copyright © 1997 by Black Collegian, Inc. Reproduced by permission of the author.

Document 12: Brotherhood and Sisterhood for All

Coretta Scott King (1929–), widow of Martin Luther King Jr., has continued in her husband's footsteps, working to promote civil rights and human rights for all Americans. In the following comments delivered to the National Gay and Lesbian Task Force shortly after the hotly disputed 2000 presidential election, King observes that her late husband's dream of a just and equitable society applies to all Americans, regardless of race, color, creed, and sexual orientation.

I think we all need a few days to recuperate from the stress-filled election we have just experienced, but not much more, because we have a lot more work to do in our common struggle against bigotry and discrimination.

I say "common struggle" because I believe very strongly that all forms of bigotry and discrimination are equally wrong and should be opposed by right-thinking Americans everywhere. Freedom from discrimination based on sexual orientation is surely a fundamental human right in any great democracy, as much as freedom from racial, religious, gender, or ethnic discrimination.

My husband, Martin Luther King Jr., once said, "We are all tied together in a single garment of destiny . . . an inescapable network of mutuality. . . . I can never be what I ought to be until you are allowed to be what you ought to be." Therefore, I appeal to everyone who believes in Martin Luther King Jr.'s dream to make room at the table of brotherhood and sisterhood for lesbian and gay people.

In addition to this fundamental moral principle, there is a very practical reason why people involved in human rights should support each other and work together. And that reason is that the whole of us united makes us stronger than the sum of our parts. This principle of synergy is eloquently summed up in the equation "One plus one equals three." In other words, there are things we achieve together that we can't achieve separately.

In a way, we have just had an object lesson in the power of coalition unity. And I think we have just seen the future of American democracy flash before our eyes last Tuesday. The coalition that gave Al Gore a popular majority can surely be as powerful as the New Deal coalition that transformed America in an earlier era.

So what comes next for the NGLTF [National Gay and

Lesbian Task Force], the King Center, and indeed all organizations working for human rights and social justice must be a new emphasis on working together in coalitions. With this commitment, we can pass comprehensive hate crimes legislation and the Employment Non-Discrimination Act and secure full funding for AIDS research, prevention, and treatment. We can defend affirmative action and support a broad range of common legislative and policy priorities.

It is encouraging that we have seen more gay and lesbian candidates elected to political office. It is important for lesbian and gay officeholders and their constituencies to achieve greater visibility as supporters of laws that benefit the entire community. I think this will help educate the American public that lesbian and gay people seek the same goals of quality education for young people, cleaner air and water, safe streets and better health care that straight people want. We have to work harder for the broader vision of the compassionate and caring society that demands decent living standards for all citizens.

Now that the election is finally behind us, we must turn our full attention to building a tightly knit coalition of human rights groups that can act swiftly and effectively for needed policy reforms. Let's make this first decade of the 21st century an era of unprecedented expansion in freedom and democracy.

And as we work for needed reforms, we must also look ahead to the next elections, mindful that we need more people of color in America's federal, state, and local political institutions. And we also need more women and more lesbian and gay officeholders as well. This is how we make our political institutions reflect the diversity of the American people.

In closing, my friends, I just want to say that I'm proud to stand with you today as we build a great new American coalition for freedom and human rights for all people. Despite the formidable challenges we face, I believe that we will succeed in creating a more compassionate and just society.

I'll conclude my remarks tonight with a few words spoken by Martin Luther King Jr. at the National Press Club in July of 1962. The 38 years that have come and gone since then have done nothing to diminish the relevance of his remarks. Indeed, they seem particularly appropriate to the challenge we face today.

"We are simply seeking," said Martin, "to bring into full realization the American dream—a dream yet unfulfilled. A dream of equality of opportunity, of privilege and property widely distributed; a dream of a land where men no longer argue that the color of a man's skin determines the content of his character; the dream of a land where everyone will respect the dignity and worth of the human personality—this is the dream. When it is realized, the jangling discords of our nation will be transformed into a beautiful symphony of brotherhood, and men everywhere will know that America is truly the land of the free and the home of the brave."

With this faith, sisters and brothers, let us work together with renewed passion and commitment to create the beloved community of Martin Luther King Jr.'s dream, where all people can live together in a spirit of trust and understanding, harmony, love, and peace.

Document 13: America's Forgotten Citizens

In the following selection from a 2003 Children's Defense Fund statement, Marian Wright Edelman calls attention to the ongoing problems of unemployment, hunger, and homelessness among America's urban poor, and calls on policy makers in the Bush administration and Congress to do more for the disadvantaged.

The U.S. Conference of Mayors released its 18th annual "Status Report on Hunger and Homelessness in America's Cities." The mayors' report was an urgent reminder of how many families are struggling mightily to keep food on the table and a roof over their heads. It found that hunger and homelessness rose sharply over the last year in the twenty-five cities surveyed while resources to meet these needs declined. In every city, the mayors expect requests for both emergency food assistance and shelter to increase during 2003. Freezing temperatures and budget cuts have created a significant rise in homelessness and hunger.

I believe if you want to work, you ought to be able to find a job. And if you are working, you ought not to live in poverty. Yet nearly forty percent of the adults surveyed who requested food assistance and more than one in five homeless adults were employed but still just couldn't make ends meet.

Our stereotypical image of a homeless person or someone in a soup kitchen line is not usually a child. But children often constitute a large part of the face of hunger and homelessness in our country. Forty percent of the homeless population in survey cities were families with children, and half of those requesting emergency food assistance were families with children. Many had to be turned down because cities did not have enough resources to go around. Imagine being the parent in one of those families. How would it feel returning from a food pantry to face your hungry children empty-handed? And how must it feel when a family has no place to sleep or has to be split up in order to receive shelter? Nearly forty percent of families' requests for emergency shelter simply went unmet.

Why is there no room for our children in our 21st-century inn in the wealthiest nation on earth? Why are our political leaders cutting the heating and shelter and child care and child health assistance children desperately need while squandering hundreds of billions of dollars on tax cuts for millionaires?

City officials believe there are a number of reasons why hunger and homelessness are rising across the country. They cite high housing costs as the leading cause of hunger, followed by unemployment, low wages, and the economic downturn. They believe lack of affordable housing is also the leading cause of homelessness, followed by low-paying jobs, substance abuse, mental illness, domestic violence, and unemployment. Yet the United States Senate voted in January to cut programs to reduce substance abuse and help the mentally ill, and the Bush administration dragged its feet in extending unemployment compensation benefits until after

Christmas. We forgot that there are real human beings behind every statistic—people like Mrs. Arlene Cruz, a 55-year-old grandmother struggling to care for the four grandchildren she rescued from foster care and whose plight was chronicled by the *New York Times*.

Mrs. Cruz tried valiantly to deliver the children to their Manhattan public schools starting from a different homeless shelter each day. She worked at a low-wage supermarket job but was unable to get a voucher for child care because she was not on welfare. She tried to make ends meet by adding a shift as a hospital aide. When her health failed, the family fell deeper and deeper into a bottomless pit without a home. Should Mrs. Cruz and the more than two million grandparents like her struggling to keep families together lack the support they need—especially when foster care and homeless shelters cost taxpayers so much more than decent child care and housing assistance? Are the hurdles Mrs. Cruz was forced to overcome in order to survive and keep her grandchildren together the best this nation can do? I don't think so. It's time to stand up to leaders who say we cannot afford to feed and house our children but can afford to fund a war against Iraq and to spend billions to prepare for a Star Wars missile defense system when children face the daily terrors on earth of abuse, neglect, violence, poverty, and preventable sickness.

For the first time, the mayors' report calls on the federal government to take specific actions, including "building upon President Bush's request for aid to the homeless, as part of a comprehensive effort to end homelessness within ten years," "enact[ing] a national housing agenda . . . which would put thousands of Americans to work," and "streamlin[ing] anti-hunger programs." We can and must make ending disgraceful hunger, homelessness, and child poverty a national priority. The grandparents and parents struggling to hold their families together would agree that food and shelter and a job are the most urgent homeland security issues they face.

Marian Wright Edelman, *Hunger and Homelessness: The Real Homeland Security Issues*. Washington, DC: Children's Defense Fund, 2002. Copyright © 2002 by Children's Defense Fund. All rights reserved. Reproduced by permission.

For Further Research

Books

Herbert Aptheker, *Abolitionism: A Revolutionary Movement.* Boston: G.K. Hall and Twayne, 1989.

Kathleen M. Blee, ed., *No Middle Ground: Women and Radical Protest.* New York: New York University Press, 1998.

Taylor Branch, *America During the King Years, 1954–63.* New York: Simon and Schuster, 1988.

Robert Brisbane, *Black Activism: Racial Revolution in the United States, 1954–1970.* Valley Forge, PA: Judson Press, 1971.

Elaine Brown, *A Taste of Power: A Black Woman's Story.* New York: Pantheon Books, 1992.

Ellen Cantarow, Susan Gushee O'Malley, and Sharon Hartman Strom, *Moving the Mountain: Women Working for Social Change.* Old Westbury, NY: Feminist Press, 1980.

Nancie Caraway, *Segregated Sisterhood: Racism and the Politics of American Feminism.* Knoxville: University of Tennessee Press, 1991.

Clayborne Carson, *In Struggle: SNCC and the Black Awakening of the 1960s.* Cambridge, MA: Harvard University Press, 1981.

Septima P. Clark, *Echo in My Soul.* New York: E.P. Dutton, 1962.

Bettye Collier-Thomas, *Daughters of Thunder: Black Women*

Preachers and Their Sermons, 1850–1979. San Francisco: Jossey-Bass, 1998.

Bettye Collier-Thomas and V.P. Franklin, eds., *Sisters in the Struggle: African American Women in the Civil Rights–Black Power Movement.* New York: New York University Press, 2001.

Vicki L. Crawford, Jacqueline A. Rouse, and Barbara Woods, eds., *Women in the Civil Rights Movement: Trailblazers and Torchbearers.* Brooklyn, NY: Carlson, 1990.

Dwight Lowell Dumond, *Antislavery: The Crusade for Freedom in America.* Ann Arbor: University of Michigan Press, 1961.

Sara Evans, *Personal Politics: The Roots of Women's Liberation in the Civil Rights Movement and the New Left.* New York: Alfred A. Knopf, 1979.

V.P. Franklin, *Black Self-Determination: A Cultural History of African-American Resistance.* Brooklyn, NY: Lawrence Hill Books, 1992.

Paula Giddings, *When and Where I Enter: The Impact of Black Women on Race and Sex in America.* New York: William Morrow, 1984.

LaVerne McCain Gill, *African American Women in Congress: Forming and Transforming History.* New Brunswick, NJ: Rutgers University Press, 1997.

Fannie Lou Hamer, *To Praise Our Bridges.* Jackson, MS: KIPCO, 1967.

Nancy Harrison, *Winnie Mandela.* New York: George Braziller, 1985.

Darlene Clark Hine, ed., *Black Women in American History: The Twentieth Century.* Brooklyn, NY: Carlson, 1990.

Joy James, *Shadowboxing: Representations of Black Feminist Politics.* New York: Broadway Books, 1998.

June Jordan, *Fannie Lou Hamer.* New York: Crowell, 1972.

Susan Kling, *Fannie Lou Hamer: A Biography.* Chicago: Women for Racial and Economic Equality, 1979.

Aileen Kraditor, *Means and Ends in American Abolitionism.* New York: Ivan R. Dee, 1989.

Steven F. Lawson, *Black Ballots: Voting Rights in the South.* New York: Columbia University Press, 1976.

Chana Kai Lee, *For Freedom's Sake: The Life of Fannie Lou Hamer.* Chicago: University of Illinois Press, 1999.

Manning Marable, *Race, Reform, and Rebellion: The Second Reconstruction in Black America, 1945–1982.* Jackson: University of Mississippi Press, 1991.

Doug McAdam, *Freedom Summer.* New York: Oxford University Press, 1988.

Kay Mills, *This Little Light of Mine: The Life of Fannie Lou Hamer.* New York: Dutton, 1993.

Anne Moody, *Coming of Age in Mississippi.* New York: Dial Press, 1968.

Pauli Murray, *Pauli Murray: The Autobiography of a Black Activist, Feminist, Lawyer, Priest and Poet.* Knoxville: University of Tennessee Press, 1989.

Lynne Olson, *Freedom's Daughters: The Unsung Heroines of the Civil Rights Movement from 1830 to 1970.* New York: Scribner, 2001.

Nell Irvin Painter, *Sojourner Truth: A Life, a Symbol.* New York: W.W. Norton, 1996.

Charles Payne, *I've Got the Light of Freedom: The Organizing Tradition and the Mississippi Freedom Struggle.* Berkeley: University of California Press, 1995.

Jane and William Pease, *They Who Would Be Free: Blacks' Search for Freedom, 1830–1861.* New York: Atheneum, 1974.

Jane Rhodes, *Mary Ann Shadd Cary: The Black Press and Pro-*

test in the Nineteenth Century. Bloomington: Indiana University Press, 1998.

C. Peter Ripley, ed., *Witness for Freedom: African American Voices on Race, Slavery, and Emancipation.* Chapel Hill: University of North Carolina Press, 1993.

Belinda Robnett, *How Long? How Long? African American Women in the Struggle for Civil Rights.* New York: Oxford University Press, 1997.

Columbus Salley, *The Black 100: A Ranking of the Most Influential African-Americans, Past and Present.* New York: Citadel Press, 1994.

Jessie Carney Smith, ed., *Notable Black American Women.* 2 vols. Detroit: Gale Research, 1992, 1996.

Dorothy Sterling, *Black Foremothers: Three Lives.* New York: Feminist Press/McGraw-Hill, 1979.

Jeannie Swift, ed., *Dream and Reality: The Modern Black Struggle for Freedom and Equality.* Westport, CT: Greenwood Press, 1991.

Wendy Hamand Venet, *Neither Ballots nor Bullets: Women Abolitionists and the Civil War.* Charlottesville: University Press of Virginia, 1991.

Robert Weisbrot, *Freedom Bound: A History of America's Civil Rights Movement.* New York: Norton, 1990.

Deborah Gray White, *Too Heavy a Load: Black Women in Defense of Themselves, 1894–1994.* New York: Norton, 1999.

Jean Fagan Yellin and John C. Van Horne, eds., *The Abolitionist Sisterhood: Women's Political Culture in Antebellum America.* Ithaca, NY: Cornell University Press, 1994.

Howard Zinn, *SNCC: New Abolitionists.* Boston: Beacon Press, 1964.

Document Collections and Other Primary Sources

Alfreda M. Duster, ed., *Crusade for Justice: The Autobiography of Ida B. Wells.* Chicago: University of Chicago Press, 1970.

Marian Wright Edelman, *Lanterns: A Memoir of Mentors.* Boston: Beacon Press, 1999.

Suzanne Pullon Fitch and Roseann M. Mandziuk, *Sojourner Truth as Orator: Wit, Story, and Song.* Westport, CT: Greenwood Press, 1997.

From Slavery to Freedom: The African American Pamphlet Collection, Library of Congress, Rare Book and Special Collections, Washington, DC.

Winnie Mandela, *Part of My Soul Went with Him.* New York: W.W. Norton, 1984.

Deirdre Mullane, ed., *Crossing the Danger Water: Three Hundred Years of African-American Writing.* New York: Anchor Books, 1993.

Richard Newman, Patrick Rael, and Philip Lapsansky, eds., *Pamphlets of Protest: An Anthology of Early African American Protest Literature, 1790–1860.* New York: Routledge, 2001.

C. Peter Ripley et al., eds., *The Black Abolitionist Papers: Vol. I: The British Isles, 1830–1865.* Chapel Hill: University of North Carolina Press, 1985.

Ida B. Wells-Barnett, *On Lynchings.* Salem, NH: Ayer Company, 1991.

For Internet Research

American Memory: Historical Collections for the National Digital Library, Library of Congress, http://memory.loc. gov/ammem/amhome.html. The Library of Congress's American Memory collection is an invaluable electronic archive of primary documents significant for the study of American history, politics, and culture. American Memory provides access to over 7 million digital items, including the African-American Pamphlet Collection, a vast archival resource of original documents concerning slavery, abolition, and the struggle for freedom.

The American Passages: A History of the United States, www.wadsworth.com/history_d/special-features/ext/ap/ MainAP/allchapters.html. Online companion to the textbook with representative primary and secondary materials focusing on pivotal moments in American history from the colonial days through the Clinton presidency.

Documenting the American South, an electronic archive of southern history, literature, and culture, http://metalab. unc.edu/docsouth. Documenting the American South offers a wealth of primary documents relevant to the American southern experience from colonial times to the early twentieth century. It is an especially good source for slave narratives and other rare first-person narratives (memoirs, diaries, letters, travel writing).

Douglass Archives of American Public Address, http://pubweb. northwestern.edu/~doetting/douglass.htm. Named for Frederick Douglass, this electronic archive published by Northwestern University contains speeches from 1645 through the present dealing with important social, political, and historical issues in the United States representing a host of eminent politicians and public figures.

Index